CW01655109

Original title: Pintxos de leyenda de Donostia (2016 Ttarttalo)

© Text: 2016, Josema Azpeitia Salvador
© Translation: 2016, Katy Ryan
© Images: 2016, Diaporama Estudio Foto
© For this edition: 2016, Ttarttalo S.L.

Cover and design: Unai Arana
Layout: Eneko Maiz

ISBN: 978-84-9843-687-7
D.L.: SS-268-2016

Ttarttalo argitaletxea
Portuetxe, 88 bis
20018 Donostia
Tel: 943 31 02 67

ttarttalo@ttarttalo.eus
www.ttarttalo.eus

Printed by: Leitzaran Grafikak, S.L. Martin Ugalde Kultur Parkea, Andoain (Gipuzkoa)

Famous pintxos
OF
DONOSTIA - SAN SEBASTIÁN

Josema Azpeitia

TTARTTALO

San Sebastián
a living pintxo museum

Just as pasta is from Italy, sushi is from Japan and fish and chips are from Britain or wieners are from Frankfurt, pintxos, wherever they are made, are from San Sebastián. The pintxo (pronounced 'pincho') was invented in San Sebastián – at first they called them *banderillas* after the barb used in bullfighting, also a tradition here –, evolved in San Sebastián and has undergone a revolution in San Sebastián to become what it is today; a gastronomic phenomenon with creativity, freedom and innovation which is a far cry from the initial narrow definition of a slice of French bread and 2 or 3 bites to eat on top. Nowadays the pintxo can be found in all shapes, forms, dishes, colours, smells and tastes.

The custom of 'going out for pintxos' was invented in San Sebastián too; going from bar to bar sampling the speciality or newest creation of each establishment, accompanied by a small drink, whether wine, a small glass of beer or cider, and eating two or three pintxos before going to lunch or dinner - the pintxo was first designed as an appetizer or hors d'oeuvre. When pintxo bars spread and become more popular, the idea of 'having pintxos as lunch or supper' came along and also became a habit, going from bar to bar, or staying in one bar and tasting 4, 5, 6 or 7 types, or however many you could manage to eat. Then pintxo tasting menus came into fashion on the coattails of the new Basque haute cuisine, which is now seen everywhere in the bars and restaurants in the city.

San Sebastián too saw the creation, to our shame, of the now-traditional custom of the 'plate', that platter offered to a visitor to fill up with all the pintxos they want (the more the merrier); pintxos which they often cannot finish and which kill their desire to go on and try other bars and other pintxos. This is a tourist trap, a *feast today, famine tomorrow* of the restaurant industry which has become the key difference between good and bad pintxo bars.

The first pintxo

So, as you can see, the pintxo is an eminently San Sebastián phenomenon, and here in this picture-postcard city is where it all began. It is commonly accepted that the starting point was the simple combination of an olive, some pickled green chilli peppers and a salted anchovy, and that the bar Casa Vallés (now in Reyes Católicos street, then still a wine warehouse in Isabel la Católica street) was the place where a playful client, Joaquín Aranburu, alias "Txepetxa", started to thread the three ingredients onto a toothpick, creating the first *banderilla*. This was the 'Gilda', named in honour of the film starring Rita Hayworth; this was first shown in cinemas here in 1946, and for the people of San Sebastián at the time the film was, like the pintxo, "saucy and hot".

Some people argue about this story, and it is true that everyone knows that someone must probably have put these three ingredients together in many places before the Casa Vallés did so, and not necessarily in San Sebastián. However, anecdotal and historical circumstance have come together in this bar, and we have the creator's name too, so 'officially' the original pintxo was created here.

Pintxos and tapas

In whatever way it was created, the Gilda combines several features which have traditionally defined the pintxo and which differentiate it from what was known as a 'tapa' until then. For a start, the Gilda is an independent culinary preparation. It is not a serving of a larger dish (like a paella, omelette or stew) on a plate; it is not a slice of something (cured meat or cheese) on a piece of bread. It is an individual concoction with various ingredients, tastefully put together to provide a specific sensation in the mouth. It is a miniature dish.

Also, you eat the Gilda in your hand and in one, two or three bites, which is the characteristic that used to be the *sine qua non* that defined the pintxo until evolution did away with this feature. Another essential thing is that it has to be skewered onto a cocktail stick, which explains why it is called a 'banderilla' or 'pintxo', both meaning a type of spike or stick.

Finally, as the most important feature, you pay for the Gilda. The big difference, enormous for some, between a pintxo and a tapa is that you pay for the former and the latter is free. The pintxo, since the beginning, has involved work, experimentation in the search for flavours and the use of fresh products in its preparation that should logically be paid for.

Accepting these initial premises as a fact was how San Sebastian started to fill up with pintxo bars; timidly at first and en masse by the end of the twentieth century. The pintxo phenomenon grew between the 40s and 90s and spread to other places in Gipuzkoa and to the main Basque cities, and after the boom of the early twenty-first century, the phenomenon spread beyond the Basque borders and settled in the rest of Spain and beyond. It was renamed 'tapa' with a few honourable exceptions in other parts of Spain but, as I explained at the beginning, it should be called the 'Pintxo of San Sebastian' here and everywhere.

San Sebastián, a pintxo museum

As San Sebastián is the capital where this culinary and social phenomenon was created, a place where gastronomy is an almost religious passion and a place where tradition and respect for a product are almost as important as innovation, it is a city that can offer us something we cannot find anywhere else in the world; a journey through the history of pintxos where we can taste, today, some of the most emblematic specialities of this creation over the different decades of its existence, in the bars where they were created, and cooked and served by the people who devised them, or by their descendants. This is the route we invite the reader to take in *Famous Pintxos of Donostia – San Sebastián*.

The first chapter of the book is called 'Pioneers'. Not only have the five bars in this chapter been open for more than five decades; they were also in business at the time when pintxos began to appear in the bars of San Sebastián, and are still run by the same people and the same families. They continue to produce the same legendary pintxos that made them famous.

So to start, we can go to Casa Vallés to eat the original Gilda. Then 200 metres further on at La Espiga, we can taste their Chorreras or their delicious Morritos. Then, in the Old Town, we can visit the Casa Tiburcio (this bar is nearly a hundred years old) to enjoy a classic pintxo at its imposing bar, and in Paco Bueno we must not leave without trying the Medio huevo egg pintxo, which has been made there every day in exactly the same way since the bar opened in 1950. To finish on a high note, we will go to the area of the city called Gros, where the charismatic Ezkurra bar continues to delight customers with its Russian salad; this pintxo was already revered in the 1960s and has never changed its recipe.

We can take this same route, this joy to the palate and the senses, in what I consider to be the different stages that the San Sebastian pintxo has known; innovation in the 80s and 90s, the revolution that happened in the early twenty-first century and the new and the fresh ideas that new cooks are contributing today around a format in which virtually everything has been invented. We finish with a tour of the suburbs, to show that pintxos are not only to be found in the tourist or business areas of the city (Old Quarter, Centre and Gros); we claim that there is life out there, that in every corner of San Sebastián we can find a bar that, without necessarily being an establishment that specialises in pintxos, will always have one or more miniature marvels that will sate your appetite.

You choose; you can use *Famous Pintxos of Donostia - San Sebastián* as a recipe book, to re-create the miniature jewels in the crown of San Sebastián's gastronomy at home, tailored to your own taste, expertise and pocket. You can use it as a guide for five themed tours that show separate moments in the pintxo phenomenon. Or you can opt for a historical tour, starting with the oldest bars and ending with the newest. The book also makes other suggestions in 'You may also enjoy...', in addition to the 25 main bars listed. It is a dynamic, multi-use book, which I hope will satisfy whoever buys it with a practical use in mind, not just to add another pretty book to their shelves.

San Sebastián is a living museum of pintxos and *Famous Pintxos of Donostia - San Sebastián* was designed to be the best guidebook and companion for anyone who wants to explore it and enjoy the taste experience. Come, see ... and enjoy!!

Josema Azpeitia. Food critic.
Legazpi, 6th February 2016.

Xabier Gutiérrez

PINTXOS: A BITE TO READ

PIONEERS

"Mum, I want that Russian salad pintxo," said the child, standing on tiptoes at the bar to point.

"Okay, but don't get it all down you. I'll get it. Wait a minute."

The woman chose the largest one from the trays crowding the long bar top. All the colours and shiny food looked delicious. She handed it to her son with a paper napkin and the glass of juice with its squirt of soda water was left on the table while the boy ate carefully. First, with his fingers, he ate the prawn from the top of the pintxo. His mother took the stick from her own pintxo, potato omelette, and began to eat too.

INNOVATORS

"How much have you got?"

"Only fifteen pesetas," answered the teenager.

"That's enough. I've got ten pesetas. If we put them together, it's enough for two pintxos and a small beer.

"And how do we share that between the three of us?"

"Easy, dammit. Like we always do. We stand in the corner next to the door and each take one from the bar. Of course, trying to do it just when nobody's looking. That is important. Don't ask the waiter for anything hot. If we do that, we'll get caught.

"And then, one of us pays for two pintxos and a small beer. You sneak out when you have eaten yours. Like always," he repeated.

"Bloody hell, one day we are going to get caught," replied one of them. "And just one small beer between three of us, that's useless."

REVOLUTIONARIES

"Look, this is the Church of San Vicente and this is the oldest street in San Sebastián. 31 de Agosto Street."

"Okay, right, but we are going to eat something, aren't we? Less sightseeing; take us on a pintxo tour, because we haven't come five hundred kilometres in a bus to see stones."

"Here, in here," he said, pointing to one of the closest bars.

The two couples entered the bar.

"Hi there, two beers and two wines. What new pintxos have you got?"

"There, on the board. We put them up last week. They are all new," answered the waiter.

Anchovy with spider crab, Mackobe, Iron Maiden Squid, Txupa Txup Cod à la Pil-Pil, Millefeuille of smoked eel.

"Bloody hell, we don't understand anything," said the guests.

"Don't worry, I'll order," said the host.

The aromas of the pintxos began mixing with flavours and with grateful smiles.

"They were delicious," said the guests leaving the bar. "So, let's go for lunch now, shall we?"

The hosts rolled their eyes in disbelief.

NEW ARRIVALS

"That's amazing!" exclaimed the blonde with high heels. "Who would have thought it? A burger bar in the middle of the Old Quarter. Fantastic!"

"No, darling. We are not in Melbourne now. I want to eat pintxos, remember?"

The couple kissed as if they had just met. The Australian boyfriend was even better-looking than the woman herself.

When they finished snogging they looked around them in the Boulevard in San Sebastian. They opened the map and pointed to it, trying to work out where they were. They walked until they got to the bar.

"Are you sure this is the place?" asked the blonde.

"I think so," answered her boyfriend.

They began to read the menu carefully.

"Teriyaki Chicken. Three-piece sushi. Avocado makis. Sea bass sashimi."

HIDDEN

"Every day there are more tourists in this city. You can't just go out for a drink, dammit."

"Yeah, it's awful. Any day they will throw us out of our own city."

"Heck, you can hardly move in summer. Look how busy the old quarter is already, and it's only May," answered the third friend.

"Times have changed. And not for the better!"

The eight friends entered the next bar.

"Yes?"

"Eight small wines."

"I love this place more and more each time. Patxi's is the best bar. And nobody knows about it.

"Yeah, but it could do with a lick of paint."

"Hey, we've had several rounds without eating a thing. Bring out some battered prawns, Patxi."

"And some potato omelette," called another.

"Coming up!"

Xabier Gutiérrez.
Head Development Chef at the Arzak restaurant and writer.
San Sebastián, 20th January, 2016. San Sebastián Day.

Pioneers

CASA VALLÉS · LA ESPIGA · CASA TIBURCIO
PACO BUENO · EZKURRA

Everything has a beginning, and pintxos are no exception. The Gilda of Casa Vallés is considered the first San Sebastian pintxo - although some argue that it is not - and 1946, the year of the premiere of the film that gave it its name, is the year in which it was created, or at least baptised.

However, after 1946 it would be many years until the bars in San Sebastián were filled to overflowing with '*banderillas*', a name with clear bull-fighting connections referring to a toreador's spike, which was used at first to refer to the pintxos. The 50s and 60s were the decades when this custom really got going; small portions of food presented on a piece of bread started to occupy the bar counters to the point that

sometimes it was difficult to find a space at the bar to put your glass down.

Bars at that time looked different too; any place worth its salt had several dozen hams hanging above the bar, a product that was not common in private homes and therefore was consumed in great quantity in the city's watering holes. In some cases, such as Casa Vallés or other emblematic establishments like La Cepa, the consumption of ham outstripped that of most establishments in the rest of Spain, including in the cradle of Iberian ham itself, Andalusia. The bars were larger and roomier then, the counters higher and the usual furniture was long tables and benches.

For this chapter, we have selected five bars that opened in the 40s and 50s (or even earlier) that are not only still open today but are managed by the same families that ran them in the mid twentieth century. They are, without doubt, the living history of the San Sebastian pintxo.

DON'T MISS:

LA CEPA
31 de Agosto, 7. Old Quarter

CASA ALCALDE
Nueva, 19. Old Quarter

IZKIÑA
Fermín Calbetón, 4. Old Quarter

GORRITI
San Juan, 3. Old Quarter

INTZA
Esterlines, 12. Old Quarter

BAZTAN
Puerto, 8. Old Quarter

BODEGA DONOSTIARRA
Peña y Goñi, 13. Gros

SAN MARCIAL
San Marcial, 50. Centre

LA CUEVA
Plaza de La Trinidad. Old Quarter

MESÓN MARTÍN
Elkano, 7. Centre

Casa Vallés

Reyes Católicos, 10. Centre. Tel. 943 45 22 10

OPENED IN 1942

Blas Vallés, from Olite in Navarre, moved to San Sebastián in 1942 to found Casa Vallés; at first it was a warehouse selling Navarran wine but within a few years it became a bar-restaurant, and since then, the same family has continued to run this classic San Sebastián establishment. Casa Vallés still embodies the essence of the old days better than any other bar with its hanging hams, its long tables, its food orders shouted loudly and its numerous prompt, professional waiters. It has survived two fires, in 1973 and 1986, and Casa Vallés proudly boasts the invention of the Gilda pintxo.

Gilda

INGREDIENTS (MAKES 1 PINTXO):

1 green olive
5 pickled chilli peppers
1 Cantabrian anchovy
Sunflower oil
1 cocktail stick to hold the pintxo together

Remove the stalk from the chilli peppers and string them onto the cocktail stick, placing them alternately so that each one faces a different side.

The order of ingredients is as follows: first the olive, then the chillies and finally the anchovy, folded double, next to the end of the stick used to pick up the Gilda.

Drizzle the Gilda with a little olive oil.

This pintxo, with its simple but intense flavour, is thought to be the first ever San Sebastián pintxo. It is said that it was created in Casa Vallés around 1946, when a customer, Joaquín Aranburu, nicknamed 'Txepetxa', threaded the three ingredients onto a cocktail stick and called it a 'Gilda' in tribute to the film released that year, which, like the pintxo, was 'saucy and hot', according to Vallés customers.

Spanish Omelette with Cod

INGREDIENTS:
Soaked salt cod
Eggs
Onion
Green pepper
Olive oil

Sauté the onion and green pepper in olive oil very slowly, so they do not burn, and try to keep the pepper *al dente*.

Once the vegetables have sautéed, add the cod in fairly large pieces, covering the base of the frying pan. Do not use pieces of cod that are too small or they will turn to a paste.

Beat the eggs in a bowl and pour the cod and vegetables into the eggs. Mix well and cook the omelette in a clean frying pan over a high heat. When the eggs begin to solidify, turn it by placing a plate on top; flip the pan over, slide the omelette back into the pan and continue cooking the underside.

Grilled Squid

INGREDIENTS:
A medium-sized squid
Mashed potato

FOR THE VINAIGRETTE:
Carrot
Green pepper
Onion
Extra virgin olive oil
Vinegar

FOR THE VINAIGRETTE: Dice the carrot, green pepper and onion and mix with the olive oil and vinegar. This is better if made in advance.

FOR THE MASHED POTATO: Cut the potatoes into small pieces and fry them slowly in olive oil on a low heat. Drain the oil off, mash them with a fork and add a little salt.

Clean the squid carefully, leaving the skin on. Pat dry and place on a very hot griddle or grill and sear the squid, turning frequently until it is done.

PRESENTATION: Spoon the mashed potato onto a plate as a base, then place the squid on top and drizzle the vinaigrette over it.

Jabugo Ham on Toast

INGREDIENTS:
1 slice of Jabugo ham
1 slice of French bread
Extra virgin olive oil
One tomato

Cut a generous slice of bread and toast it.
Pour a good dash of extra virgin olive oil over it.
Grate the tomato onto the slice of bread
Cover the toast with a large slice of Jabugo ham.

Although it is simple, this ham on toast is one of the most popular products at Casa Vallés. Good Jabugo ham has always been one of the hallmarks of the bar since it opened in 1942.

Tuna with anchovy and chilli pepper

INGREDIENTS:

1 or 2 pieces of Albacore tuna in olive oil
3 or 4 pickled green chilli peppers
1 large salted Cantabrian anchovy

Spread the tuna out on a plate, loosely piling the flakes on top of each other so that they cover the plate.

Remove the stalk from 3 or 4 pickled chillies and place the chillies on top of the tuna.

Top the dish with the large salted Cantabrian anchovy and drizzle with olive oil.

Finally, add a drop of vinegar to taste.

Casa Tiburcio

Fermín Calbetón, 40. Old Quarter. Tel. 943 42 31 30

OPENED IN 1929

Entering Casa Tiburcio at 11 am, when it has just opened its doors and is empty, is an amazing experience. It's like a leap into the past, with its wooden walls, large tables and its high, elegant bar where the bright, freshly prepared pintxos shine in their dozens, waiting for the customer to pick them up as they have always done. Tibur Eskisabel continues the dynasty that began nearly a century ago with his grandfather, Tiburcio. His is a cuisine of succulent flavour, where dishes like Cod à la Pil-pil, Cod cheeks in Green sauce or Stewed Squid are prepared with the utmost respect for tradition, although Tibur does not skimp on modern touches, which led him to win the Pintxo Championship of Gipuzkoa, 2015.

Tuna with vinaigrette

INGREDIENTS (MAKES 1 PINTXO):
1 large cube of tinned Olasagasti tuna in brine
1 olive stuffed with green chilli pepper
Parsley

FOR THE VINAIGRETTE:
Onion
Green bell pepper
Conserved red piquillo pepper
Salt
Extra virgin olive oil
White wine vinegar

First, prepare the vinaigrette by chopping the onion, green pepper and red pepper finely in a bowl and mixing them together in the following approximate proportions: 50% onion, 30% green pepper and 20% red pepper. Mix everything with the olive oil, white wine vinegar and salt and set aside.

PRESENTATION: Thread the stuffed olive and a cube of tuna onto a long skewer. Place the skewer on a plate and cover with the vinaigrette.

Sprinkle with freshly chopped parsley.

This is one of the oldest pintxos in the Casa Tiburcio, from before the time that Tibur Eskisabel joined the kitchen staff, and it is still very popular at the bar.

Tuna in onions

Winner of the Pintxo Championship of Gipuzkoa, 2015

INGREDIENTS (MAKES 15 PINTXOS):

15 cubes of fresh Albacore tuna
2 onions
2 cloves garlic
Soy sauce
Fish stock
Chives
Extra virgin olive oil
Salt
Black pepper

FOR THE REDUCTION OF MODENA VINEGAR:

Balsamic vinegar
Sugar

Cut the tuna into triangular wedges, add salt and pepper and marinate them for 10 minutes in a mixture of soy sauce and fish stock.

Remove the tuna wedges from the marinade, put them into another bowl and cover them with extra virgin olive oil. Store them in the fridge overnight.

To present the pintxo, prepare the onion and garlic; cut the onions into julienne strips and chop the garlic finely. Heat the olive oil in a pan and add the onion while the oil is still cold. Bring the heat up, then lower it and simmer the onion for about an hour, adding the chopped garlic in the last 10 minutes when the onion is almost done.

To make the reduction of of Modena vinegar, put 5 parts of vinegar to 1 of sugar in a saucepan. Leave it on a medium heat for about 30 minutes or until it has reduced to the desired consistency.

PRESENTATION: To serve the pintxo, take the tuna from the fridge, thread it onto a skewer and grill it on a hotplate like a steak, leaving the inside raw and pink.

Serve the tuna in a bowl, adding some onion on top. Sprinkle with chives and finish off with a drizzle of reduction of Modena.

Cod confit on grilled vegetables and teardrop peas in green sauce

INGREDIENTS (MAKES 1 PINTXO):
1 cube of cod 3x3 cm
2 large pieces of bread crust
Extra virgin olive oil

FOR THE VEGETABLES:
Onion
Aubergine
Green pepper
Garlic
Salt

FOR TEARDROP PEAS IN GREEN SAUCE:
Gipuzkoan teardrop peas
Extra virgin olive oil
Garlic
Parsley
Flour
White wine
Salt

FOR THE VEGETABLES: Bake the vegetables in the oven for an hour at 180° C. Once done, peel and cut them into thin strips and add a pinch of salt. Cut the garlic into slivers, fry them in olive oil until brown and pour them over the vegetables strips.

FOR THE TEARDROP PEAS IN GREEN SAUCE: Heat oil in a frying pan or casserole dish. Add sliced garlic and, when it starts to fry, add the chopped parsley. Add uncooked teardrop peas, then a little flour and salt and stir. Add a little white wine, bring to the boil and simmer for a few minutes for the alcohol to evaporate.

Toast the bread crusts in the oven for a few minutes.

Confit the cubes of cod by cooking for three minutes in olive oil over a low heat.

PRESENTATION: To serve the pintxo, put a tablespoon of grilled vegetables in a bowl. On top of them, place the two toasted bread crusts. Then place the cod confit on top and finish the dish with the teardrop peas in green sauce.

This pintxo was created by Tibur Eskisabel for the first Cod Pintxo Championship of Gipuzkoa, held in 2015.

Grilled cod with fried vegetables

INGREDIENTS (MAKES 4 PINTXOS):

4 thick slices salt cod
1 leek
½ onion
1 green pepper
1 red pepper
½ potato
2 cloves garlic
1 small carrot
4 slices French bread
Olive oil

REDUCTION OF MODENA VINEGAR:

Balsamic vinegar
Sugar

Cut the salt cod into cubes of equal size and thickness so that they cook evenly.

Brown the cod in a frying pan and then finish it on a hot griddle.

Cut the vegetables into julienne strips and fry in plenty of hot olive oil.

Prepare four slices of fried bread; fry them in very hot olive oil, but for a very short time, so that the bread is not too crunchy.

PRESENTATION: Assemble the pintxo by arranging a slice of bread on a plate, and drizzling it with the cooking juices from the cod. Place the cod on the bread and then the fried vegetables on top.

Finish the pintxo with a few trickles of reduction of Modena vinegar.

To make the reduction of Modena, put 5 parts of vinegar to 1 of sugar in a saucepan. Leave it on a medium heat for about 30 minutes or until it has reduced to the desired consistency.

Black pearl

INGREDIENTS (MAKES 1 PINTXO):
3 thick flakes of tinned tuna
Half a slice of tomato
Parsley
1 pickled onion marinated in reduction of Modena vinegar

FOR THE REDUCTION OF MODENA VINEGAR:
Balsamic vinegar
Sugar

FOR THE VINAIGRETTE:
Onion
Fresh green pepper
Conserved red piquillo pepper
Salt
Extra virgin olive oil
White wine vinegar

Before making this pintxo, place a lot of pickled onions in a jar and cover with reduction of Modena vinegar (see recipe for Grilled cod). Let the onions macerate for several days until they turn a dark, almost black, colour.

PRESENTATION: To present the pintxo, cut a slice of French bread and place the half slice of tomato on it.

Cover the tomato with three slices of tuna. This is a product that can be found in delicatessens such as La Koxkera in the Old Quarter of San Sebastian by asking for 'morrillo o cogote de bonito'.

Pour several spoonfuls of vinaigrette over the tuna, prepared as in the recipe for Tuna à la vinaigrette.

Finish the pintxo with an onion marinated in Modena vinegar, to make a "Black Pearl".

This is a recently-created pintxo, cool and ideal for summer, though its popularity means that it can be found in Casa Tiburcio throughout most of the year.

Ezkurra

Mirakruz, 1. Gros. Tel. 943 27 13 74

OPENED IN 1960

Ezkurra is a living example of a family exodus, when the Balda family left Betelu (Navarre) in the 60s and came to try their luck in the Gipuzkoan capital. The Baldas moved from the country to the city, setting up the Ezkurra and giving it a real family atmosphere. Joseba Balda, the third generation to run the business, recalls his grandparents in the kitchen while their children managed the bar, kitchen and supply work. This was when the recipe for the Russian salad pintxo was created, and it has not changed one jot in over half a century; it remains the hallmark of this meeting point for the people of Gros.

Russian salad

INGREDIENTS (MAKES 1 PINTXO):

Potato
Egg
Carrot
Tinned peas
Tinned tuna
Salt
Bread

FOR THE MAYONNAISE:

Egg
Extra virgin olive oil
Vinegar
Salt

FOR THE MAYONNAISE: Put an egg in a mixing bowl. Add salt and begin to beat with a stick blender. While beating, add the olive oil very slowly, keeping a steady trickle going, and the mayonnaise will gradually acquire the desired consistency. At the end, still beating, add a few drops of vinegar.

Cook each of the ingredients separately: the potato and the carrot for half an hour and the egg for 15 minutes.

Let them cool, then peel, chop and mix together in a bowl. Then add the peas and tuna. Add salt to taste and stir the mixture well.

PRESENTATION: Cut a slice of bread, put a good spoonful of Russian salad onto it, add the mayonnaise and garnish the top with grated hard-boiled egg-white.

Foie gras with apple purée

INGREDIENTS (MAKES 1 PINTXO):
1 fresh slice of foie gras
Maldon salt

FOR THE APPLE PURÉE:
1 cooking apple
Sugar
Water

FOR THE APPLE PURÉE: Peel and cut the apple into small cubes. In a saucepan, heat the sugar and add a little water to make the caramel. Once it is golden brown, add the diced apple.

Stir the apple vigorously with a wooden spoon for about five minutes, to absorb all the sugar.

When the apple is golden brown, mix it in a food processer to a purée.

Fry the slice of foie gras quickly in a hot pan.

PRESENTATION: Place a tear-shaped drop of the apple purée on a saucer with a spoon. On that tear-drop, put the foie and sprinkle it with Maldon salt.

Smoked salmon roll

INGREDIENTS:

Smoked salmon
Bread
Butter
Mayonnaise
Parsley

FOR THE TARTARE SAUCE:

A pickled cucumber
Black olive
Onion
Green pepper
The white of a hard-boiled egg
Mayonnaise

FOR THE TARTARE SAUCE: Chop all the ingredients very fine. Mix well and add the mayonnaise.

Butter a piece of toast and heat it on a hotplate or griddle. On top, place the fillet of smoked salmon, filled with tartare sauce and shaped into a roll.

PRESENTATION: Garnish the pintxo with a line of mayonnaise and sprinkle freshly chopped parsley on top.

Mushroom risotto with foie gras

INGREDIENTS:

Rice	Fresh foie gras
White wine	Bread
Onion	Butter
Mushrooms	Parsley
Cream	

Cook the rice as normal but two or three minutes before the end of the cooking time, add a glass of white wine and let it evaporate. Set aside the cooked rice.

Meanwhile, chop the onion and fry it gently. When it is done, add the mushrooms and let them soften well too.

Add the cream and let it reduce. Then blend everything and add the cooked rice. Sauté the rice and add more cream, depending on the creaminess you want.

PRESENTATION: Fry the slice of foie gras in a hot pan and chop it up. Add the pieces of foie to the risotto with some breadcrumbs fried in butter. Finally, sprinkle with chopped parsley.

Mushrooms in filo pastry

INGREDIENTS:

Filo pastry	Butter
Mushrooms	Nutmeg
Milk	Red wine
Flour	Strawberry jam

Finely chop the mushrooms, sauté and prepare a béchamel sauce with flour, milk and butter to which you add the mushrooms. Add a pinch of nutmeg.

Once the béchamel is cool, take the filo pastry squares and fill them with the mushroom béchamel, rolling them closed like a spring roll.

Fry the rolls in olive oil.

PRESENTATION: Prepare a coulis to decorate the rolls. To do this, reduce red wine, add strawberry jam, reduce again and strain.

Draw a few trickles with the coulis on the filo pastry rolls before serving.

La Espiga

San Marcial, 48. Centre. Tel. 943 42 14 23

OPENED IN 1928

La Espiga is forever fixed in my gastronomic memory. This is the first place I remember ever having eaten a pintxo, back in the '70s when my parents came to San Sebastián. Even then, the bar, which was high for a youngster of 8 or 10, overflowed with pintxos. Now, the amounts of pintxos are more modest and most of them have to be ordered from the kitchen, like its famous dish of beef snouts. Founded in 1928, today it is run by the grandchildren, and was fully renovated in 2007. It is one of the bars with the biggest contrast between its appearance, which is modern and functional, and its selection of pintxos, which remains as traditional as ever, with products such as *Txorrera* or *Jalisco*, which form part of the gustatory memory of San Sebastián.

Fried artichoke

INGREDIENTS:

1 artichoke
Water
Salt
Olive oil
Parsley oil

Boil the artichoke whole in salted water without removing any leaves, for about 20-25 minutes.

Once cooked, let the artichoke cool and begin to remove the outer leaves until you are left with only the heart.

Cut the artichoke in half and immediately deep-fry it.

When lightly browned, drain the artichoke, place it on a saucer and garnish with parsley oil.

Beef snout in sauce

Best Traditional Recipe in the Alcorta-Martín Berasategui Competition, 2007

INGREDIENTS:
2 beef snouts
1 carrot
1 onion
1 sweet red pepper
Flour
Egg
Salt

FOR THE SAUCE:
3 carrots
3 onions
White wine

In a saucepan, sauté the onions and carrots over a low heat diced into mirepoix.

Put cook the snouts, carrot, onion and red pepper into a pressure cooker and cook for 45 minutes after bringing to the boil.

Remove from heat and remove the snouts (leaving the vegetables and stock in the pot). Drain and cool the snouts.

Add the sautéed onions and carrots to the remaining stock in the pot. Add a splash of white wine to taste and add salt. Blend with a stick blender and set aside.

Cut the snouts into small squares, more or less one centimetre thick.

Dip in egg, dust with flour and fry in hot oil.

Add the snouts to the sauce, bring to boil and simmer for 10 minutes.

For each pintxo, serve 2 or 3 generous pieces of snout accompanied by the sauce.

* The snouts are bought and cooked whole. They are fillets cut from the area of the cow's cheeks.

Leftover tuna and prawns

INGREDIENTS:
Tinned tuna
Courgettes
Onion
Piquillo peppers
Spicy paprika
Tomato sauce
Rosemary
Bay leaf
Puff pastry tartlets
Cooked prawns
Chilli threads

Sauté the courgettes and the onion in julienne strips. When the vegetables start to soften, add a sprig of rosemary and a couple of bay leaves.

Add the crumbled tuna and tomato. Cut the piquillo peppers into strips and add.

Finally, add the paprika, bring everything to the boil and cook for 3 minutes.

PRESENTATION: Fill a puff pastry tart with the sauté and put a peeled shrimp and a few strands of chilli thread on top.

Pintxo of ratatouille with anchovies

INGREDIENTS:
Anchovies
Vinegar
Oil
Salt
Soy sauce
Bread
Garlic

FOR THE RATATOUILLE:
Onion
Red pepper
Green pepper
Courgette
Vine tomato

FOR THE RATATOUILLE: Cut the vegetables into regular pieces. Put the onion and green pepper in a pan to fry followed by the red pepper, tomato and the courgette. Let them sauté for a long time.

When the vegetables are cooked, remove them from the pan and reduce the juice remaining in the pan.

When the pan juice is reduced, add the vegetables again and add salt.

FOR THE MARINATED ANCHOVIES: Put the anchovies in a large bowl, add vinegar to cover them, a glass of water and a handful of salt.

Stir them carefully so that they are all equally salted and let them marinate for about three hours.

PRESENTATION: Fry a rectangular piece of bread and drain it well. Cover the bread with ratatouille and place an anchovy on top. Add a little soy sauce and a pinch of fried garlic and parsley.

To preserve the anchovies after marinating them, cover them with sunflower oil and finely chopped raw garlic).

Pintxo delight

INGREDIENTS:
Salted anchovies
Hard-boiled egg
Onion
Parsley
Mayonnaise
Vinegar
Oil
Salt

On a slice of French bread, place two salted anchovies at the edges. Put a little mayonnaise between the two anchovies.

Cut the boiled egg into thin slices, cut one of the slices in half and place it in the middle of the pintxo.

Finally, fill the sides of the pintxo with vinaigrette and garnish with a little more mayonnaise on top of the egg.

Paco Bueno

Mayor, 6. Old Quarter. Tel. 943 42 49 59

OPENED IN 1950

Paco Bueno was a mythical boxer who decided to hang up his gloves and go into the restaurant business; it went so well for him that his son, also called Paco Bueno, and his family still run this mythical bar where you come to eat freshly-made Battered Prawns, Croquettes or Stuffed Peppers. "The secret? Good, fresh ingredients, freshly made every day," is what they never tire of repeating in this old bar. It has kept its original appearance almost intact, and at the bar you can taste famous pintxos such as the Half Egg, a pintxo which, Paco says, "has been made every day since we opened in 1950."

Battered prawns

INGREDIENTS (MAKES 1 PINTXO):

2 prawns
Baking powder
Egg
Flour
Beer
Salt
Water
Olive oil

Mix the flour, baking powder, a dash of beer, salt, water and egg in a large bowl and mix well.

The single biggest secret of this pintxo, and many others of this restaurant, is to work the batter for the prawns really well. Mix it for a long time so that there are no lumps, getting the ideal texture for coating the prawns.

Once the batter is ready, peel the prawns except for the tail, to use as a handle for coating them and when eating.

Dip the prawns generously in the batter, and fry them in very hot clean olive oil.

Serve the pintxo to eat immediately before it cools.

Paco Bueno salad

INGREDIENTS:
Tomato
Potato
Egg
Tuna in olive oil
Asparagus
Prawn
Olives stuffed with anchovies

FOR THE VINAIGRETTE:
Onion
Tomato
Green pepper
Extra virgin olive oil
Salt
Vinegar
White wine
Balsamic vinegar

Cut the tomato into slices. Boil the potatoes and egg and cut into slices. Cook the prawn and peel it.

Finely chop the ingredients of the vinaigrette and mix thoroughly until emulsified. Let the mixture stand, if possible overnight.

Put the ingredients in this order on a plate; the slice of tomato, slice of potato, slice of boiled egg, a piece of tuna in olive oil, half an asparagus and the peeled prawn. Stick a cocktail stick through them to hold it all together and top it with an olive stuffed with anchovy.

Finally, pour the vinaigrette generously over the top.

Half egg

INGREDIENTS (MAKES 2 PINTXOS):

1 boiled egg
Tuna in olive oil
Mayonnaise
Bread

Cut the hard-boiled egg into two equal halves and separate the yolk from the white.

Finely chop the egg yolk and mix it in a bowl with the tuna and mayonnaise. There should be much more tuna proportionally than the other ingredients.

Cut a slice of French bread of about the same surface area as the egg, about 2 centimetres thick.

Stuff the hollow of the egg white with the mixture of tuna, egg yolk and mayonnaise, and put it upside down on top of the slice of bread.

Garnish the egg with a dot of mayonnaise and stick a toothpick through the whole pintxo.

The half egg is a historic pintxo which has been prepared in the Paco Bueno bar every day since it opened in 1950.

Spoon salad

INGREDIENTS (MAKES 1 PINTXO):

1 peeled prawn
½ an asparagus
1 slice of smoked salmon
1 small piece of avocado
Vinaigrette (see recipe for the for the Paco Bueno Salad)

Spear the following ingredients onto a toothpick in the following order: a cooked peeled prawn, a slice of avocado, half an asparagus and a slice of smoked salmon folded in half.

Place this brochette horizontally on a special spoon for pintxos.

Dress the pintxo with the vinaigrette used in the Paco Bueno Salad recipe.

Stuffed Pepper

INGREDIENTS:

Whole cooked red peppers
Iberian ham
Minced meat
Spring onion
Green pepper
Olive oil
Batter (see Battered Prawns recipe)

Finely chop the onion and green pepper and sauté them in a pan with a little olive oil.

When they are cooked, add a little chopped ham, sauté for a few minutes and add the meat. Fry until the meat is cooked.

Put the mixture in a bowl and mash together to get a paste.

Fill the red peppers with this mix, then dip each one in the batter and fry in hot olive oil.

At the Paco Bueno bar we also make some great peppers stuffed with crab, following virtually the same recipe, although without ham.

Innovators

BERGARA • GARBOLA • ITURRIOZ HAIZEA • HIDALGO 56

The first boom in pintxo bars took place in the 80s and 90s as a direct consequence of the creation of New Basque Cuisine. Several bars begin to experiment with the extended pintxo format, taking it to new heights of culinary excellence, without it losing its main original features; to be picked up in one hand and eaten in a few bites.

The pintxo turned into a product that was often called "miniature haute cuisine" but was still presented at the bar on a slice of bread or toast. Those in charge of these innovative bars became true gastronomic engineers, racking their brains about how to make world-class authentic creations in such a small format. They also began to use unusual ingredients for bars,

such as homemade smoked products, foie gras or sea urchins.

This was the time when the first talks, competitions and events featuring pintxos began to be held and we started hearing the names José Ramón Elizondo, Patxi Bergara or Mikel Santamaría in the media. Revolutionary bars like the Oñatz, Aloña Berri and Negresco also became temples of pintxos, but they unfortunately closed later, perhaps because they were too ahead of their time.

As in the previous chapter, we have selected four bars belonging to that stage which are still open, run by the same cooks or their relatives or descendants, as well as a fifth bar, Hidalgo 56, which, although more modern, is the natural continuation of the now defunct bar Hidalgo, which in the years covered in this chapter renewed its cuisine and gained a Michelin star.

DON'T MISS:

GANBARA
San Jerónimo, 21. Old Quarter

TAMBORIL
Pescadería, 2. Old Quarter

TXEPETXA
Pescadería, 5. Old Quarter

ANTONIO
Bergara, 3. Centre

IOMBI
Plaza de Gipuzkoa, 15. Centre

MARTÍNEZ
31 de Agosto, 13. Old Quarter

ROJO Y NEGRO
San Marcial, 52. Centre

LA VIÑA
31 de Agosto, 3. Old Quarter

ESPARRU
Carlos I, 16. Amara

URDIÑOLA
Carlos I, 16. Amara

Bergara

General Artetxe 8, on the corner of Bermingham. Gros. Tel. 943 27 50 26

OPENED IN 1950

The Bergara opened in 1950, but its most radical renovation began in 1982 when Patxi Bergara took over and made it one of the most famous pintxos bars in the city. In 1991, he won the First Pintxo Championship of San Sebastián with the Cocktail Bergara, also known as the *Txapeldun*, whose recipe appears in this book. Today, famous pintxos such as the False Anchovy Lasagne or the Duck Delight with Calvados are still popular in the Bergara, although the third generation is not resting on its laurels and has done wonders with such pintxos as its Raf Tomato Hamburger, its Ratatouille Gratin with Mushrooms and its Tinned *Fideuá*.

Anchovy omelette

INGREDIENTS (MAKES 12 PINTXOS):

6 eggs
18 gutted anchovies
1 slice of cayenne pepper
1 large clove garlic
Olive oil
Salt
12 slices of bread

Peel and chop the garlic and the anchovies into very small pieces. Beat the eggs. Fry the garlic in olive oil until brown. Add the cayenne pepper, sauté it a little with the garlic, and add the anchovies. Almost immediately, add the beaten eggs and salt. Stir the omelette as it sets, making sure it doesn't dry out.

PRESENTATION: Divide the omelette into 12 triangular portions, put each on a slice of bread and serve on a plate.

Even though it is very simple to make, anchovy omelette is one of the most popular pintxos in the Bergara Bar, with its flavour and melt-in-the-mouth texture, and it is one of the classics of this bar.

Txapeldun
(Cocktail Bergara)

First prize in the I Pintxo Championship of San Sebastián, 1991

INGREDIENTS (MAKES 18 PINTXOS):
6 slices of fresh pineapple
12 prawns
1 cooking apple
5-6 slices of bread

FOR THE COCKTAIL SAUCE:
Mayonnaise
Tabasco
Ketchup
Brandy

FOR THE COCKTAIL SAUCE: Mix the mayonnaise and ketchup in equal quantities in a bowl. Add a dash of tabasco and a dash of brandy, according to taste or intentions (the tabasco makes it spicy and cognac gives it a kick).

Drain the pineapple and dice into small cubes. Chop the prawns into small pieces, 4-5 mm. thick.

Peel the cooking apple, core it and chop it into tiny pieces, even smaller than the pineapple chunks and shrimp.

Put everything together in a bowl and add the cocktail sauce to taste.

PRESENTATION: Toast the slices of bread and cut them into portions for each pintxo (each slice will make 3-4 servings, depending on the size of the pintxos). Place a dollop of the mixture on each slice making a pile and crown it with a little more cocktail sauce to make it pretty.

The Txapeldun is well known for being the Bergara Bar's first pintxo to win a prize in the Pintxo Championship of San Sebastian in the 90s. The bar won many other award subsequently.

Tinned noodles with prawn and squid

INGREDIENTS
Vermicelli noodles
Prawns
Squids
Red bell pepper
Green pepper
Onion
Garlic
Cayenne chilli pepper
Olive oil

FOR THE FISH STOCK:
Fish bones
Prawn shells and heads
Water

FOR THE AIOLI:
Extra virgin olive oil
Garlic
Milk

FOR THE FISH STOCK: Put the fish bones with the shells and heads of the prawns to cook over a low heat for at least two hours.

FOR THE LIGHT AIOLI: Mix or whisk finely-chopped garlic, extra virgin olive oil and a dash of milk in a bowl.

FOR THE NOODLES: Fry the uncooked noodles with a little olive oil. When they start to brown, strain the oil set them aside.

Meanwhile, dice the peppers, onion and garlic and sauté in a pan with olive oil. Add a little cayenne pepper, chopped prawns and baby squid and and sauté everything together for a while. Finally, add the noodles and fish stock and bring to the boil. When the noodles stiffen upwards, it means that they are done.

PRESENTATION: Fill a tin with a generous portion of the noodles and garnish with two teaspoons of aioli. Present the noodles in the can with its lid propped up beside it.

The fideuá was one of the dishes that the Bergara team regularly included in their set menus without meaning to prepare it as a pintxo. It was Elena Arzak who encouraged those responsible for the bar to give it a try. To their surprise, it went down a storm and today is one of the most popular pintxos at the bar.

Ajoarriero

INGREDIENTS (MAKES ABOUT 16 PINTXOS):

4 salt cod fillets
1 large potato
1 large onion
1 large green pepper
1 dl tomato sauce
16 prawns
3 cloves garlic
Olive oil
Salt
Bread

Soak the salt cod for 24 hours, changing the water three times, every 8 hours. Drain, dry, remove the skin and bones and break it up into medium-sized pieces.

Peel and dice the potatoes.

Heat a frying pan over a low heat with about 2.5 dl. olive oil. When hot, add the potatoes, turn down the heat very low and let them cook slowly, not letting the oil bubble, turning them occasionally. When they are soft, add salt and mash them a bit with a fork until they are almost broken up. Remove from the heat and drain the oil away completely.

While the potatoes are cooking, boil the prawns in a separate saucepan in salted water for half a minute. Take them out, peel them and cut each into three equal pieces.

Place a clay dish over a low heat with a little oil, onions and green peppers, all finely chopped. Leave to cook slowly until everything begins to brown. At that point, add the flaked cod, mix with a wooden spoon and cook for about three minutes. Then, add the drained potatoes, bits of prawn, tomato sauce and the finely chopped garlic. Add a dash of the oil which the potatoes were cooked in and cook for three or four minutes, stirring continuously with a wooden spoon.

PRESENTATION: Remove from the heat and for each pintxo serve a couple of tablespoons of *ajoarriero*, accompanied by a slice of bread.

Juan Mari Arzak has always been a great fan of this ajoarriero, which is often eaten with a spoon, like a soup.

Duck delights with calvados

INGREDIENTS (MAKES ABOUT 15 PINTXOS):

1 duck breast
1 large cooking apple
2 cloves garlic
1 glass Calvados
45 pine nuts
15 puff pastry tartlets
Butter
Salt
Pepper

Cut the duck breast first into thin slices and then into cubes about 5 mm thick.

Peel and core the apples and chop them into even smaller pieces than the duck.

Peel the garlic and chop into very small brunoise cubes.

Heat a pan with butter and sauté the pieces of duck breast in it; it will release quite a lot of fat. At that point, add the chopped garlic and apple and cook everything together for a few minutes. When everything is soft and sautéed, add the glass of Calvados and bring it to the boil so that the alcohol evaporates.

Toast the pine nuts in a hot pan.

PRESENTATION: Spoon the mixture into small puff pastry tartlet cases and top each with three freshly roasted pine nuts.

Garbola

Paseo Colon, 11. Gros. Tel. 943 28 50 19
OPENED IN 1992

Pintxo innovation in Gros must include Gregorio Martínez, who combines his interest in gastronomy with a passion for cocktails. Since its start in the 80s, the Garbola has innovated pintxos with the introduction of toast, smoked pintxos and special croquettes, and Gregorio suggests pairing with cocktails, prepared flawlessly and usually made to suit the customer's tastes. To understand the audacity of this barman, barman, you have to know that Gros was a neighbourhood of garages, workshops and pubs that served large sandwiches. Gregorio brought a breath of fresh air to this scene and today, in the twenty-first century, he is famous in the world of liquid alchemy.

Pistachio croquette

INGREDIENTS:

Pistachios	Salt
Prawns	Flour
Spinach	Milk
Onion	Egg
Olive oil	Breadcrumbs

Cook the spinach in a saucepan in lots of salted water. Let it cool and chop finely. Set aside.

Dice the pistachios, onion and prawns. Sauté the onion. Add the pistachios and prawns and sauté everything together. Add the chopped spinach, then the flour and then the milk, and make a béchamel or white sauce, stirring the mixture constantly.

Once the béchamel thickens up, allow it to cool and shape it into croquettes. Dip the croquettes in egg, coat them in breadcrumbs and fry them in olive oil until golden brown and crispy on the outside.

Shark pintxo

INGREDIENTS:
Fillet of shark
Potatoes, cut into thick rounds
Onion
Green peppercorns
Olive oil
Sherry
Salt

Fillet the shark to remove any bones and fry with green peppercorns and a dash of sherry.

Fry the potatoes in a separate pan.

Chop the onion into julienne strips and sauté until caramelized.

Put one or two slices of potato on a plate, place a slice of shark on top and garnish it with onion and green pepper with the scent of sherry.

This pintxo is exotic and goes well with any tropical cocktail served in the bar, such as a refreshing Mojito or Caipirinha, which Gregorio Martínez makes with authentic Brazilian cachaça.

Tuna with chives and parsley

INGREDIENTS:
Tuna in olive oil
Spring onion
Parsley
Mayonnaise
Salt
Bread

Toast a slice of bread and place a generous slice of tuna in olive oil on it.
Finely chop the fresh chives and place them on the tuna.
Make a classic mayonnaise with egg, olive oil, salt, vinegar and lemon juice and spoon a tablespoon of it onto the chives.
Sprinkle the pintxo with freshly chopped parsley.

Because of its lavour and aroma, this is a pintxo that goes well with a Dry Martini, the famous cocktail popularized in the 1970s by James Bond. It is a classic cocktail that Gregorio Martinez makes to perfection in the Garbola and he will make it to the client's taste.

Kangaroo with cream of mushrooms

INGREDIENTS:
Kangaroo fillet
Assorted mushrooms
Onion
Carrot
Green pepper
Leek
Potato
Olive oil
Salt

Fry the kangaroo fillet in olive oil for a few minutes and set aside.

FOR THE MUSHROOM SAUCE: Finely chop the onion, carrot, green pepper and leek. Sauté them all in olive oil over a low heat. When browned, add the chopped mushrooms and sauté everything together for several minutes until the mushrooms are tender. Put some mushrooms aside to decorate the pintxo at the end and blend the rest in a food processor, and strain.

FOR THE POTATOES: Cut the potatoes into thick slices and cook them in olive oil over a low heat for 5-10 minutes until they go golden brown.

PRESENTATION: Place two or three potatoes on a small tray. Place two pieces of kangaroo fillet on top and cover with mushroom sauce. Garnish with the whole cooked mushrooms.

Anchovies with egg threads and tomato confit

INGREDIENTS:
Salted anchovies
Mayonnaise
Egg
Dried tomato confit in olive oil
Bread

Cook the egg for 10 minutes, let it cool, peel, remove the yolk and grate it into threads. Set aside.

Toast a slice of bread and cut to size for this one-bite pintxo.

Place two salted anchovies on the slice of toast.

Make a classic mayonnaise with egg, olive oil, salt, vinegar and lemon juice and put a little mayonnaise on the toast.

Place a slice of dried tomato confit in olive oil on the mayonnaise and sprinkle the pintxo with the grated egg threads.

Haizea

Aldamar, 8. Old Quarter. Tel. 943 42 57 10
OPENED IN 1982

Although it is separated from the Old Quarter by the Bretxa Market, the fact that this bar is slightly hidden has not prevented the Haizea from attracting great chefs like José Juan Castillo or Juan Mari Arzak among its clientele. The latter had the bright idea of bringing Anthony Bourdain, the American 'travelling chef' to eat here. Bourdain presented it on one of his programmes and turned Mitxel Ibáñez into the most famous San Sebastián waiter in the United States. The owners, Maite and Iñaki Agote, virtually never come out of the kitchen, where they have been cooking little works of art for decades. If you come to the Haizea, ask for their seasonal pintxos and don't forget to try their famous tongue sandwich.

Fresh foie gras with apple

INGREDIENTS (MAKES 1 PINTXO):
1 slice of foie gras
Salt
1 cooking apple
Water
Sugar

FOR THE APPLE PURÉE
Apple
Water
Sugar

Cut two thin slices of apple and set aside.

With the rest of the apple, make a purée: cut the apple into small pieces, boil it in water with sugar (a little less sugar proportionally than water) and simmer for half an hour. Blend in a food processor and strain.

Leave the two thin slices of apple in water with sugar for 4 hours or more. Then put them in the oven on baking paper and bake for half an hour at 150° C. When they come out of the oven they will be soft, but they will immediately harden on cooling.

Cook the slice of foie gras on a hot griddle or pan, turning various times, and sprinkle with a little salt.

PRESENTATION: Place a couple of tablespoons of apple purée in the centre of a hot plate. Place one of the thin slices of apple on the purée, and on top of this, the hot foie gras. Cover the foie gras with the second slice of apple and garnish the pintxo with another spoonful of apple purée.

Prawn stuffed with crab in American sauce

INGREDIENTS:
1 large king prawn

FOR CRAB STUFFING:
Crab meat
Onion
American sauce
Cream

FOR THE AMERICAN SAUCE:
Onion
Leek
Carrot
Tomato
Prawn heads
Prawns
Norway lobster tails
White wine
Water
Salt
Pepper

FOR THE AMERICAN SAUCE: Chop and fry the onion, leek, carrot and tomato. When sautéed, add the prawn heads, some small whole prawns and, optionally, some Norway lobster tails.

Sauté well until the shells brown, add the white wine and water and cook for about an hour until soft.

Add salt and pepper, blend in a food processor and strain.

FOR THE CRAB MEAT: Break up the crab meat, removing all the bones.

Fry the finely chopped onion, add the crab meat and sauté.

When cooked, add the American sauce and boil for a few minutes.

When serving the pintxo, add a little cream and reduce.

PRESENTATION: Peel the prawn, cut it in half lengthwise and cook quickly on a very hot griddle or pan, turning various times.

Place in the centre of the plate, cut side up, and pour the crab meat and American sauce over it.

Stuffed mini crab

INGREDIENTS (MAKES 1 PINTXO):
1 clean empty small crab shell
Onion
Flaked crab meat
Brandy
Flour

FOR THE AMERICAN SAUCE:
Onion
Leek
Carrot
Tomato
Prawn heads
Prawns
Norway lobster tails
White wine
Water
Salt
Pepper

FOR THE AMERICAN SAUCE: Chop and fry the onion, leek, carrot and tomato. When sautéed, add the prawn heads, some small whole prawns and, optionally, some Norway lobster tails.

Sauté well until the shells brown, add the white wine and water and cook for about an hour until soft.

Add salt and pepper, blend in a food processor and strain.

PRESENTATION: Sauté a little diced onion and add the flaked crab meat, a little brandy and a spoonful of flour. Mix this with the American sauce and spoon the mixture into the crab shell, presenting it like a mini baked crab.

Scallop and prawn brochette

INGREDIENTS (MAKES 1 PINTXO):

1 scallop
2 prawns
Olive oil

FOR THE TARTARE SAUCE:

Mayonnaise
Pickled gherkin
Capers
Hard-boiled egg
Spring onions

FOR THE TARTARE SAUCE: Dice the gherkin, capers, boiled egg and spring onions. Mix into the mayonnaise. Set aside, if possible overnight as this sauce tastes better if it is given time to rest.

PRESENTATION: Thread a scallop and two prawns onto a cocktail stick and grill them. Once done, add a drizzle of good extra virgin olive oil. Serve with the tartare sauce.

Optionally, garnish this pintxo with a lettuce leaf.

Mushrooms in sauce

INGREDIENTS:
Mushrooms
Garlic
Olive oil
Salt
Pepper
Stock
Flour
Cayenne pepper oil

Dice the garlic and fry it in olive oil. Add the mushrooms whole, add salt and pepper and let it sauté.

Cover the mushrooms with stock and simmer for about 40 minutes.

Drain the mushrooms, pass them to another saucepan with a little of the cooking stock, add a spoonful of flour, bring to the boil again, stir and then take off the heat.

PRESENTATION: Before serving, add a few drops of cayenne pepper oil.

Hidalgo 56

Paseo Colon, 15. Gros. Tel. 943 27 96 54

THE ORIGINAL HIDALGO, OPENED IN 1956. THE CURRENT HIDALGO, OPENED IN 2005

Hidalgo 56 is the family continuation of the Hidalgo bar, which is now closed. It was there, watching his mother, Silvi Hidalgo, that Juan Mari Humada caught the cooking bug, and it was there, in 1993, that the Michelin Guide awarded him a star. Juan Mari Humada has been creating small wonders for a lifetime and they have won him big prizes in competitions in Gipuzkoa and the Basque Country. His son, Sergio Humada, head chef at the Vía Veneto in Barcelona, is continuing the family tradition at the highest level.

Autumn Pintxo

INGREDIENTS (MAKES 1 PINTXO):
3 mushrooms
2 chestnuts
1 free-range egg yolk
2 cloves garlic
Sunflower oil
Maldon salt
Chives

FOR THE CHESTNUT CREAM:
Chestnuts
Milk
Salt
Pepper

FOR THE GAME STOCK:
Venison bones
Onion
Leek
Carrot
Olive oil
Red wine
Water

FOR THE GAME STOCK: Peel and chop onion, leek and carrot into large pieces. Roast in the oven at 220° C with the deer bones and a little oil until golden brown. Put it all into a casserole pot, deglaze the tray with the venison bones and add to the pot, add water, bring to the boil and let it reduce over a low heat for a few hours. When the stock has thickened up, remove the bones and blend. It does not require salt.

FOR THE CHESTNUT CREAM: Boil chestnuts with milk, salt and pepper for about a quarter of an hour. Once cooked, blend them to a cream. Chestnuts are very floury, so test it as you blend them and add more milk if necessary.

Confit the chestnuts; fill a frying pan with sunflower oil and plunge the chestnuts into it. Cook at 80° C constantly for half an hour.

Confit the mushrooms; fill a frying pan with sunflower oil and two cloves of garlic. Add the mushrooms and cook at 80-85° C for 30-35 minutes.

PRESENTATION: Put the chestnut cream at the bottom of a bowl. Put the two confit chestnuts, two whole mushrooms and a third thinly-sliced mushroom on top. Cook the egg yolk for 10 seconds in the microwave and place it next to the mushroom. Sprinkle with Maldon salt and freshly chopped chives and pour the hot game stock over the plate.

This pintxo, newly created in late 2015, is an example, like most of the recipes presented here, of Juan Mari Humada's seasonal cuisine.

Smoked Idiazabal cheesecake

INGREDIENTS (MAKES 10 PINTXOS):
400 g Idiazabal cheese
350 g cream
Cocoa butter
Plain biscuits, such as Rich Tea or Graham Crackers
Idiazabal cheese ice cream or equivalent

FOR BERRY COULIS:
200 g fresh or frozen berries (blueberries, blackberries, redcurrants)
4 tbsp. sugar
50 ml water

UTENSILS: To make this pintxo, you will need cheese triangle shaped moulds, as well as a culinary smoking gun. You will also need an ice cream maker if you want the ice cream to be homemade. You will need a small round cheese bell with a glass cover for the presentation.

Chop the Idiazabal cheese and mix it with the cream in a Thermomix at 80° C until it melts. If you are doing this at home, dice the cheese, place it in a pan in a bain marie below 80° C, add the cream and leave it until it slowly melts.

Spoon the cream cheese into small moulds shaped like individual cheese triangles and put it in the freezer for at least two hours.

FOR BERRY COULIS: Cook the berries, water and sugar in a saucepan for 10 minutes over a low heat. Blend in a food processor and strain. Set aside.

When a pintxo is ordered, warm the cocoa butter in a saucepan. Take a cheese wedge out of the freezer, turn it out of the mould, and with the help of a toothpick, dip it in the hot cocoa butter so that a thin layer of cocoa is formed around the triangle.

PRESENTATION: Place a crushed biscuit on the base of the mini cheese board. Place the cheese triangle on top, and garnish with a spoonful of berry coulis. Place a scoop of Idiazabal ice cream next to the cheese triangle. Finally, cover the cheese with the glass bell and smoke the contents with the smoking gun. Serve immediately so that the diner can see the pintxo in the smoke before lifting the bell.

My style of artichoke with ham

INGREDIENTS (MAKES 4 PINTXOS):
For the ham stock:
Ham bones
Green leek leaves
Water

FOR THE ARTICHOKE CREAM:
Artichokes
Onion
Ham stock

FOR THE ARTICHOKE CONFIT:
4 artichokes
2 cloves garlic
Extra Virgin Olive Oil

FOR THE GRILLED ARTICHOKES:
4 artichokes

FOR THE FRIED ARTICHOKES:
4 artichokes
Extra Virgin Olive Oil
Salt
Iberian Ham

FOR THE HAM STOCK: Boil ham bones and green leek leaves for two and half hours over a low heat in a little water to make a gelatinous stock or consommé. Strain and set aside.

FOR THE ARTICHOKE CREAM: Dice onion and fry in oil in a pan.

Clean and peel the artichokes, leaving only the heart. Dice, add to the onion and sauté. Add a ladle of ham stock and let it cook for half an hour while reducing the stock. Blend to the texture of cream.

FOR THE ARTICHOKE CONFIT: Clean and peel the artichokes, leaving only the heart. Cook them whole with two peeled garlic cloves in extra virgin olive oil for 45 minutes at 80-90° C.

FOR THE GRILLED ARTICHOKES: Clean and peel the artichokes, leaving only the heart. Cook them in boiling water for about 15-20 minutes, testing with a fork to see when they are done. Remove from the water, drain them, cut them in half and fry them in a hot pan until golden brown.

FOR THE FRIED ARTICHOKES: Clean and peel the artichokes, leaving only the heart. Cut in half and cut into slices with a meat slicer. Heat olive oil and when it is very hot, fry the artichokes until crisp. Sprinkle with salt.

Dice the ham and fry it in extra virgin olive oil until crisp.

PRESENTATION: Take a rectangular slate, put the artichoke cream as a base, and on it, from left to right, one artichoke confit, two half grilled artichokes and some fried artichokes. Sprinkle the top with crispy ham and finally place a glass with ham consommé next to everything.

This pintxo is best eaten by trying out combinations together and taking sips of the ham consommé after tasting each type of artichoke.

Fondue

INGREDIENTS (FOR 1 PINTXO):
1 small piece of T-bone steak
Straw potatoes
2 green Gernika peppers
Salt
Pepper

FOR THE FONDUE SAUCE:
Idiazabal cheese
Goat cheese
Cream cheese (like Philadelphia)
Cream

FOR THE FONDUE SAUCE: Chop up the Idiazabal and goat cheese, add the same amount of cream cheese and cream, and mix in the Thermomix at 80° C until melted. If you are doing this at home, dice the cheeses, put them in a pan in a bain marie at about 80° C, add the cream and leave everything to melt slowly. If you want to make the sauce stronger, add some more goat cheese.

FOR THE STRAW POTATOES: Grate the potatoes with a conical grater, creating small threads. Immerse them in cold water to wash the starch away, drain them well and deep fry them in the hot oil until golden brown and crisp.

Season the piece of T-bone steak and grill or fry it, leaving it rare inside.

Fry the two Gernika peppers in hot oil.

PRESENTATION: On a small rectangular slate, put the T-bone steak, cut into small fillets; next to this place the straw potatoes and the two fried Gernika peppers and finally the cheese sauce in a small bowl.

The pintxo is eaten by dipping the meat in the sauce, like a fondue.

Tuna fillet with Basque wasabi, ginger and soy

INGREDIENTS (MAKES 1 PINTXO):
1 square of tuna (about 80 gr)
1 drop of olive oil

FOR THE GINGER AND SOY MARINADE:
Soy sauce
Fresh chives
Fresh ginger

FOR THE TOMATO JAM:
Tomato
Sugar
Water

FOR THE BASQUE WASABI:
3-4 Ibarra green chillies
Tempura flour
Water

FOR THE GINGER AND SOY MARINADE: Chop the spring onions and fresh ginger in equal quantities. Mix them with soy sauce and set aside.

FOR THE TOMATO JAM: Peel, dice and deseed the tomato and cook with sugar and water. Bring to the boil and let everything simmer for 45 minutes. Blend, strain and set aside.

FOR THE BASQUE WASABI: Mix tempura flour with cold water to get a paste. Dip the Ibarra chilli peppers in the paste and fry in abundant hot olive oil.

PRESENTATION: Heat a griddle and, with a drop of olive oil, sear the tuna fillet for two seconds on each sides, leaving it rare inside. Remove from the heat, cut it into four tiny fillets like the T-bone steak in the previous recipe and lay them out in a fan. Pour the ginger and soy marinade on top, place a teaspoon of tomato jam beside the tuna and chilli peppers next to it but without touching the jam, so that they don't lose their crunchy texture. This pintxo does not need salt, as the soy is salty.

Iturrioz

San Martin, 30. Centre. Tel. 943 42 83 16

OPENED IN THE 1930

The Iturrioz is a historic bar whose exact opening date has been lost in the mists of time, although there is evidence that it was already there before the Civil War. Since 1988 it has been run by Eduardo Bretón, who has turned the Iturrioz into one of the most famous tapas bars in the city, offering products that were innovative in their time, like the whole smoked salmon he placed on the bar and cut on demand, served in portions on little pieces of toast. He also participated in one of the first pintxo symposia held in Biarritz and has won awards with his fabulous Marinated Mackerel, or Anchovy stuffed with Peppers. Today, his son Ander has become the face of this business, ensuring the increasingly difficult handover to the next generation.

Grilled scallops with vinaigrette

INGREDIENTS (MAKES 1 PINTXO):

1 fresh scallop
Trout roe
Extra virgin olive oil
Sherry vinegar
Maldon salt

First, make a vinaigrette with some sherry vinegar and three parts extra virgin olive oil. Mix well and set aside.

Sear the scallop on the griddle, turning it so that it browns on both sides.

Place the scallop on a plate, pour the vinaigrette over it and add a teaspoon of trout roe on top.

Garnish with a few flakes of Maldon salt.

Smoked eel on toast

INGREDIENTS (MAKES 1 PINTXO):
2 slices of smoked eel
Cream cheese
Lime juice
1 tbsp. trout roe
1 slice crusty bread

FOR THE PESTO:
Basil
Pine nuts
Garlic
Extra virgin olive oil
Grated Parmesan cheese

FOR THE PESTO: Grind the basil, pine nuts and garlic in a mortar. Add a splash of extra virgin olive oil, emulsify it well and add the grated Parmesan cheese. Other cheeses like pecorino or even Idiazabal also work well instead of Parmesan.

Add the cream cheese to the pesto and mix vigorously with a stick blender to make a mousse.

PRESENTATION: Cut a good slice of crusty bread and spread it with the pesto and cheese mousse. Place the two slices of eel on top and on this, two teaspoonfuls of trout roe.

Squeeze lime juice over the pintxo to give it a citric lift.

Club Ranero Salt Cod

INGREDIENTS:
Salt cod
Cayenne peppers
Garlic
Extra virgin olive oil
Parsley

FOR THE RATATOUILLE:
Onion
Red pepper
Green pepper
Dried red pepper
Salt
Olive oil

Heat the olive oil in a wide saucepan and fry the cayenne peppers and garlic. When they are golden, put the pieces of cod in the pan skin-side up and turn off the heat.

Cut the onion into fine julienne strips and fry it in a separate pan. Then add the red pepper, also finely chopped into half julienne strips, and when they are sautéed, add the finely cut green pepper and finally a teaspoon of the pulp from the rehydrated dried red pepper. Mix well and add salt.

Returning to the cod, remove the garlic from the oil and make a pil-pil with the oil and the juice that the cod has leaked into the oil, by moving the pan in gentle circular motions until the sauce thickens to a mayonnaise-like consistency.

PRESENTATION: Serve the pintxo on a small plate, placing a little cod steak, covered with pil-pil sauce and garnished with a couple of tablespoons of ratatouille covering it. Finally, sprinkle with freshly chopped parsley.

Baked mackerel marinated in sherry vinegar

Award for the most popular pintxo contest from Cadena SER radio, 1992

INGREDIENTS (MAKES 12 PINTXOS):
1 mackerel approx. 1kg
Olive oil
Salt
Bread

FOR THE GARNISH:
2 onions
2 leeks
Black peppercorns
Bay leaf
Sherry vinegar
Olive oil
Salt

FOR THE GARNISH: Cut the onion and leek into julienne strips and the garlic into slices and sauté everything very gently. When the sauté turns brown, add black peppercorns, a few bay leaves and some salt. Cook over a low heat for half an hour or more, and then add a splash of sherry vinegar and leave a few minutes for the flavours to blend. Set aside in the fridge.

TO BAKE THE MACKEREL: Preheat oven to 250° C. Put the mackerel in a baking dish with olive oil and salt. When the oven is hot, bake the mackerel for 8-10 minutes (depending on the size of the fish). Allow to cool and fillet to remove the bones.

PRESENTATION: Prepare a slice of bread for each pintxo. Place a slice of mackerel on each one so as to cover the bread and cover the mackerel with the sautéed onions and leeks, garnishing with a few slices of garlic. It can also be served on a plate without bread.

Marinated duck magret

INGREDIENTS (MAKES ABOUT 8 PINTXOS):

1 duck breast
Balsamic vinegar
Soy sauce
Extra virgin olive oil
Maldon salt
Mixed lettuce
A tomato
Garlic
Salt
Oil

Slice the magret of duck into about 16 little fillets, and put them to macerate in a deep bowl with one part vinegar to two parts soy and 1/2 part olive oil. Leave the duck to marinate for 5 to 6 hours.

Wash the lettuce, cut very small and mix well before dressing with extra virgin olive oil, balsamic vinegar and salt.

Peel, deseed and crush the tomato.

PRESENTATION: Cut a slice of bread and spread it with the crushed tomato, garlic and salt. Put a handful of mixed lettuce on top.

Sear two slices of the magret on the griddle and put them on the lettuce.

Garnish with some flakes of Maldon salt.

Revolutionaries

LA CUCHARA DE SAN TELMO · ZERUKO
BORDA BERRI · NARRU · A FUEGO NEGRO

With the twenty-first century came the great revolution in San Sebastián pintxos. The trigger was the opening of La Cuchara de San Telmo, on St. Thomas' Day, the 21st December, 1999. From then on, nothing would be the same. In many cases, the pintxo disappeared from the bar and cooked pintxos became the norm; they were listed on a blackboard and had to be ordered and waited for and were then presented in dishes, bowls, cups, glasses or on designer plates. Also, they had the principles of haute cuisine applied to them and even the latest molecular cuisine.

This has also led to the pintxo becoming more expensive and, in many cases, passing the psychological barrier of 3 euros, equivalent to 500 of the old pesetas, an amount that shortly before, would have bought three or four

This, of course, made it more difficult to sustain the habit of eating pintxos before lunch or dinner.

The bars that had begun to combine a new, updated pintxo menu with a range of wines to go with them were also something that appeared at this time. The most emblematic example was the now-closed El Lagar, or even the Álex, which in its early years had a blackboard with suggestions for pairing its pintxos with an unusual wine list. Some locals even dared to experiment with the concept of a bar; A Fuego Negro brought a breath of fresh air, combining concepts such as gastronomy and hip-hop music, and also acting as a cultural laboratory.

The bars listed in this section appeared in the book *Pintxos de Vanguardia a la donostiarra* (Nº 35 in a cooking series published in 2009 by Ttarttalo), so some of their most interesting pintxos were published in that volume, which was recently reissued and is available in bookstores and on the website www.elkar.eus.

DON'T MISS:

NINEU
Zurriola Avenue, 1. Kursaal, Gros

SAN TELMO
Plaza Zuloaga. Old Quarter

ASTELENA 1960
Plaza de la Constitución. Old Quarter

VINOTECA BERNARDINA
Vitoria-Gasteiz, 6. Ondarreta

DAKARA BI
31 de Agosto, 25. Old Quarter

LA GUINDA
Zabaleta, 55. City centre

ETXAIDE 4
Etxaide, 4. City centre

CAFÉ KURSAL
Ramón Mª Lili, 2. Gros

CASA VERGARA
Mayor, 21. Old Quarter

NIKKEI
Urdaneta, 14. City centre

La Cuchara de San Telmo

31 de Agosto 28, rear. Old Quarter. Tel. 943 42 28 99

OPENED IN 1999

It had to be a Catalan who would revolutionise the pintxo. Álex Montiel, a deserter from haute cuisine who had risen to become the right arm of Martin Berasategui himself, opened this bar way back in 1999 with Iñaki Gulín from San Sebastián. Since then, nothing has ever been the same. Classic pintxos began to disappear from the bars, slates invaded the city and the pintxo made to order in front of the customer became the fashion. The best chefs in the world have visited La Cuchara, and today, running the bar by himself and in voluntary exile most of the year in the United States, Álex continues to run the kitchen of this bar from a distance, endlessly imitated but never equalled.

Roast tomato, ham and cheese salad

INGREDIENTS (FOR ABOUT 12 PINTXOS

2 kg large tomatoes
200 g smoked Idiazabal cheese
200 g Los Pedroches ham from Córdoba
Extra virgin olive oil
Salt
Pepper
Fresh oregano
Toasted bread

Grill the tomatoes with a little olive oil until the skin goes brown and starts to peel off. Peel them, place them in a pan and blend them with a stick blender. Add salt and pepper and extra virgin olive oil to taste. Leave to cool.

Bring the ham to room temperature.

With a cheese parer, cut thin slices of Idiazabal cheese.

PRESENTATION: Place 6 large tablespoons of the tomato in a bowl, and lay two rolls of ham (about 15 grams each), and about 7 thin slices of smoked Idiazabal cheese on top. Garnish with fresh oregano leaves, croutons or toasted bread and a splash of extra virgin olive oil.

Beer roast suckling pig with lemongrass mashed potatoes

INGREDIENTS (MAKES 35-40 PINTXOS):
1 suckling pig (about 6 kg)
1/2 lemon
3 cloves garlic
2 bay leaves
1 sprig thyme
Coarse salt
Pepper
1 glass beer
500 ml water

FOR THE LEMONGRASS MASHED POTATOES:
900 g potatoes
100 ml extra virgin olive oil
70 g butter
200 ml milk
150 ml water
3 stems lemongrass

FOR THE LEMONGRASS MASHED POTATOES: Cut 2 of the lemongrass stems into julienne strips, place in a saucepan with the milk and water and bring to the boil. Turn off the heat, cover the pan with a plate or cling film and leave to infuse.

Clean the potatoes thoroughly and cook them without peeling in a pan of cold water; add salt and one stem of lemongrass cut into strips.

Taking care not to break the skins, remove the potatoes from the water when cooked and peel them while still warm.

Blend the potatoes to a smooth purée. Pour the purée into a bowl, add the cold butter and whisk well. Add the olive oil, then gradually add the infused, strained lemongrass milk. Whisk vigorously, add salt and pepper and set aside.

FOR THE SUCKLING PIG: Prepare a baking sheet with a splash of olive oil, garlic, sprig of thyme, bay leaves and water.

Remove the head of the suckling pig, taking care not to cut away too much meat. Slice open with a meat cleaver and remove the hooves. Thoroughly clean any traces of blood or clots.

Season well with salt and pepper on both sides. Rub well with olive oil and lemon juice all over the skin.

Place the pig skin-side up, and roast in a low oven at 150° C for about 5 hours, taking care that it doesn't dry out.

When it starts to brown, add the beer.

Remove the suckling pig and, while still warm, remove the bones so the meat does not break up too much.

Press it into a mould, cool and cut up (one pig should make between 35 and 40 pintxos).

PRESENTATION: Serve a portion of suckling pig with a spoonful of lemongrass mashed potatoes.

Stuffed squid with onion compote

INGREDIENTS (MAKES 8 PINTXOS):

2 large squid
400 g onions
1 bunch of parsley
4 cloves garlic
Extra virgin olive oil
Grey salt
Pepper
A piece of Iberian acorn-fed bacon (100g)
1 sprig thyme

Chop the parsley, peel the garlic and mix together. Set aside in a bowl covered with extra virgin olive oil.

Peel and cut the onions into fine julienne strips.

Heat the oil, thyme and bacon in a pan. When the bacon is transparent, add the onions and fry over a medium heat until cooked through.

Clean the squid and taking care not to damage the skin, remove the fins, inner flesh and legs and land discard the ink sac and gladius.

Cut the squid's tubular body into four pieces lengthwise.

Finely chop the legs, fins and inner flesh and add to the onions. Sauté until tender.

Make shallow cuts with a sharp knife on the inside of each piece of squid tube.

Pour olive oil on the pieces of squid and grill or fry on both sides. Add a few drops of lemon juice and sprinkle with a few tablespoons of the garlic and parsley in oil. Rest a minute, and then add salt.

PRESENTATION: Fill each piece of squid with the onion and squid compote. When serving, garnish with a few drops of the garlic and parsley in oil.

Sea and mountains with octopus and veal snouts

INGREDIENTS (MAKES ABOUT 15 PINTXOS):

1 kg baby octopus
3 onions
4 cloves garlic
1 green pepper
50 ml white wine
150 ml chicken stock
300 g tomato sauce
400 g cooked veal snouts
Olive oil
Salt and pepper
500 ml sunflower oil
1 small bunch parsley leaves
2 bay leaves
100 g walnuts
1 chilli pepper

Cut the cooked veal snouts into bite-sized cubes.

Put salted water to boil, and clean the baby octopus well under cold running water.

When the water boils, cook the octopus until tender (about 30 minutes). When they are cooked, set them aside along with some of the cooking water.

Cut the onions and green pepper in brunoise cubes and peel and slice 3 garlic cloves.

Fry the garlic and chilli pepper in a pan with olive oil. When the oil starts to pick up the scents of the chilli and the garlic starts to fry, remove the chilli from the pan.

Add the onion and green pepper, sauté for about three minutes, add the octopus and the bay leaves and sauté them with the vegetables. Add a splash of white wine, let the alcohol evaporate and add the tomato sauce.

Add the veal snouts to the mixture, mix well, moisten with the snout cooking stock and simmer for about 20 minutes. Add salt and pepper. If the stew needs some liquid, use the water reserved from cooking the octopus.

Use a stick blender to blend the garlic cloves, the parsley, the walnuts and part of the sunflower oil (it should be the texture of pesto), then emulsify with the remaining oil.

When the stew is almost ready, add a few spoonfuls of the chopped garlic and parsley, let it cook for a few minutes and add salt and pepper.

PRESENTATION: Serve in small portions on a plate, garnishing the dish with a few drops of the chopped garlic and parsley on the *sea and mountains*.

Goat cheese custard with caramel sauce

INGREDIENTS:
7 egg yolks
300 g cream
200 g goat cheese
85 g sugar
1 vanilla pod
Caramel sauce

Infuse the cream with the vanilla pod by heating in the microwave for 2.5 minutes.

Mix the egg yolks with the sugar.

Place cheese and cream in the Thermomix, and beat for one minute. Add a little of this mixture to the egg yolks.

Heat the mixture of cheese and cream to 80° C for 4 minutes.

Add the yolks to this mixture at 90° C and beat with a spoon for about 2 minutes (when the mixture coats the spoon, it is ready).

Pour into a bowl and cool with ice.

PRESENTATION: Serve with a layer of liquid caramel on the surface.

Borda Berri

Fermín Calbetón, 12. Old Quarter. Tel. 943 43 03 42
REOPENED IN 2007

In the restaurant business, as in love or politics, there are break-ups, splits and renovations. Iñaki Gulín, co-founder of La Cuchara de San Telmo, and Marc Clua decided to work together in 2007, revolutionizing this little bar. Their cooking, based on honesty and tradition in products and dishes that can equal haute cuisine, has brought them great success. The slogan "Cooking here!" and the Bacalao Tripe à la Pil-pil, a Catalan-inspired pintxo introduced by Marc, have become famous at the Borda Berri, although anything on their tempting menu is delicious, and the team at the bar do an excellent job.

Basatxerri rib kebab

INGREDIENTS:
Basatxerri pork ribs
Ras el hanout
Curry
Paprika
Oil (or any kind of fat)
Salt
Apple
Gravy

Marinate the ribs well with the salt and all the spices and place them in a pan with fat at a low temperature (do not boil the fat), until the meat is very tender.

Let it cool. Drain the fat and leave the ribs in the refrigerator until they can be easily handled.

When cold, cut into portions and grill them until they are crispy. Add salt and pour gravy over them.

PRESENTATION: Accompany the kebab with apple sauce (slice apples, roast them, blend and strain the purée).

Cod tripe à la pil-pil

INGREDIENTS:
Cod tripe
Good extra virgin olive oil
Garlic
Parsley
Fish stock

Clean the tripe well and set aside.

Heat garlic oil without boiling it, to about 70° C. Leave the tripe in the oil to cook slowly until it has a silky texture.

Let it cool and remove part of the oil. At this point add a little fish stock to help thicken the *pil-pil* sauce, and add oil slowly while stirring. Stir continuously until the sauce thickens.

PRESENTATION: Sprinkle freshly chopped parsley on the tripe when it is ready to serve. (In the bar it is presented on a base of cauliflower cream made from boiled cauliflower and fried garlic blended to a purée).

Borda-Berri started with this pintxo many years ago, when nobody used these types of ingredients in San Sebastián. Today, even in Arzak they create many dishes in which cod tripe appears, and there are various tapas bars that serve pintxos which include it.

Garlic soup with squid tentacles

INGREDIENTS:

Zopako bread, or other crusty loaff
Garlic
Oil
Salt
Tomato sauce
Spicy paprika
Fish stock
Tentacles of baby squid

Cut the zopako bread into irregular pieces and fry with garlic in a pan.

When it has absorbed a lot of oil, sprinkle with hot paprika to taste, and before it burns, add a few tablespoons of tomato sauce. Fry it a little more and then pour in the fish stock to cover the bread.

Simmer the bread for one hour over a low heat.

After that, add a pinch of salt and break up the bread with a whisk or spoon.

PRESENTATION: Finally, season the squid tentacles, fry them in hot oil and put them into the soup. Serve very hot in individual clay bowls.

This is a pintxo which, for obvious reasons, is only served on the coldest days of winter in the Borda-Berri.

Grilled octopus with cauliflower and smoked quince vinaigrette

INGREDIENTS:
Octopus
Salt
Water
Cauliflower
Oil
Garlic
Quince paste
Paprika
Salt flakes

Boil the octopus in abundant salted water until tender. Remove from the water and set aside in the fridge.

Boil the cauliflower in abundant salted water.

Fry the garlic, drain the cauliflower, put both into a food processor and mix, adding garlic oil gradually until you get a light puree. Add salt to taste and set aside.

Cut the quince paste into small cubes and add paprika and olive oil.

Cut the octopus and grill it until crisp.

PRESENTATION: Use the cauliflower purée as a base, place the octopus on top and garnish with the quince vinaigrette and some salt flakes.

Crab ravioli

INGREDIENTS:

Crab meat
Crab roe
Leek
Tomato sauce
Brandy
Avocado
Lemon
Salt
Pepper
Garlic
Won ton
Sesame seeds
Tabasco sauce
Oil

Dice the leek and sauté it over a medium heat, adding salt and pepper. Flambé with brandy and add the tomato sauce.

Cook for a few minutes and then add the crab meat and roe, mixing well. Continue cooking to get a creamy texture. Leave to cool in the fridge.

For the ravioli base, make a guacamole, blending avocado with a little garlic, lemon juice and salt, mix well and set aside.

Cook won ton pasta in abundant boiling water, chill with ice water and stretch them out to fill with the crab filling. Fold over and close like ravioi.

PRESENTATION: Put a dollop of guacamole on a plate, with a space left in the middle to put a drop of tabasco sauce. Roast the ravioli until crisp and place them on top of the guacamole. Garnish with some sesame seeds.

Narru

Zubieta, 56, Hotel Niza. Centre. Tel. 943 42 33 49

OPENED IN 2007

Iñigo Peña opened his first Narru in 2007, in the district of Gros, when he was only 26, and awards came raining down on him; revelation chef in Madrid Fusión, one of the 10 best chefs in Europe, according to The Wall Street Journal and a Sun in the Repsol Guide. However, the crisis and the cost of rent, the cancer of the San Sebastián restaurant sector, led him in 2011 to these premises in the Hotel Niza. It's a lovely location, sober yet elegant, with a café overlooking the sea where you can sample his miniature cuisine which is simple, identifiable and technically impeccable. Inigo's cooking is based on products fresh from the market, with an especially good hand for rice dishes and unbudgeable honesty. "I cook what I like and what I understand, and people have to like that" is the maxim of this chef who still has much to say.

Iberian brawn with chimichurri and celeriac purée

INGREDIENTS (FOR 10 PINTXOS):
1 whole Iberian pig's head meat

FOR THE CHIMICHURRI:
1 red bell pepper
1 green pepper
3 cloves garlic
Oregano
Thyme
Ground black pepper
Extra virgin olive oil
Salt
Lemon

FOR CELERIAC PURÉE:
1 celeriac 800 g approx.
700 g cream
Peppercorns
Salt

FOR THE BRAWN: Roast the pig's head meat at a low temperature for 18 hours at 80° C.

FOR THE CHIMICHURRI: Chop all the ingredients finely, add the olive oil, salt and lemon and emulsify everything well to a sauce.

FOR CELERIAC PURÉE: Dice the celeriac and cook in the cream for 20 minutes, until it turns to purée. Add salt and pepper, blend in a food processor and strain.

PRESENTATION: Arrange some celeriac purée on a saucer. Place a portion of brawn on top and garnish with chimichurri.

Seafood paella with socarrat and aioli

INGREDIENTS (MAKES 15 PINTXOS):
For the seafood stock:
Shells and heads of prawns and shrimp
Water

FOR THE SQUID STOCK:
2 kg squid
1 onion
3 litres white wine

FOR THE RICE:
½ kg Spanish bomba rice
1 fresh spring onion
1 clove garlic
Fried tomato sauce
Saffron
Prawns
Aioli (prepared with olive oil, egg and garlic)

FOR THE SHELLFISH STOCK: Brown the prawn and shrimp shells and heads in the oven. Put them in a saucepan with water, bring to a boil and just when it starts to boil, remove the pan from the heat and strain the liquid.

FOR THE SQUID STOCK: Dice and sauté the onion. When it becomes transparent, add the chopped squid. Sauté and when they turn white, add the wine and leave for 3 to 4 hours on a low heat, without allowing it to boil, until the alcohol evaporates.

FOR THE RICE: Dice the onion and sauté. When it becomes transparent, add the peeled, chopped garlic clove, sauté until brown and add the rice. Sauté a little, add the saffron and a little tomato sauce.

Add the shellfish stock and bring to a boil, letting it cook for 7 minutes. Put the rice aside on a coldplate to stop it cooking further.

PRESENTATION: When a pintxo is ordered, put a helping of rice into a pan. Moisten with the squid bouillon and cook to the desired texture. Before serving, spread a teaspoonful of rice on a hot griddle, creating a circle of *socarrat* or burned rice. Peel and grill a prawn.

Serve the pintxo in a small bowl with rice at the bottom, the *socarrat* circle on top of the rice, the shrimp on top of it and a little aioli on the side as a garnish.

Iberian bacon, egg, red pepper and Parmesan cream

INGREDIENTS (MAKES 6 PINTXOS):
250 g of Iberian pancetta
Salt
Pepper
6 eggs
1 large red pepper

FOR THE PARMESAN CREAM:
200 g Parmesan cheese
375 g cream
375 g milk
4 g of Iota gelling agent

Add salt and pepper and cook the pancetta sous-vide at 65° C for 24 hours.

Roast the red pepper at 200° C for 20-25 minutes. When browned, remove it from the oven and keep it covered in a bowl for 10 minutes to make it easier to peel. After this time, peel and cut into strips.

Boil the eggs at a low temperature, 65° C, for 35 minutes.

FOR THE PARMESAN CREAM: Grate the Parmesan, mix it with the milk and cream and heat it until almost boiling. Strain it, add 4 grams of Iota gelling agent, blend in a food processor and set aside.

PRESENTATION: Brown the pancetta in a pan. Fry the egg on a griddle or non-stick pan, browning it on both sides.

Spoon the cream of Parmesan into the bottom of a deep dish. On top, place the strips of grilled pepper and then the pancetta and egg next to each other.

Cream of seasonal white asparagus with sautéed peas

INGREDIENTS (MAKES 10 PINTXOS):

FOR THE CREAM OF WHITE ASPARAGUS:
1 litre chicken stock
1 kg asparagus
250 g cream
1 egg yolk
10 g sugar
Salt

FOR THE SAUTÉED PEAS:
240 g of podded peas
80 g chopped spring onions
90 g of 0.4° olive oil

FOR THE CREAM OF WHITE ASPARAGUS: Bring the litre of chicken stock to a boil in a saucepan. While it heats up, peel the asparagus to get 1 kilo asparagus, and cut them into 2 cm slices. Pour the asparagus slices into the chicken stock when it comes to a boil.

Add the sugar and let it cook for 20 minutes with the lid on.

Blend in a food processor and then strain through a fine sieve. (There should be nothing in the sieve if the asparagus is totally cooked).

Put the cream of asparagus back in the pan over the heat and add the mixed egg yolk and cream.

Heat to 80° C, and immediately cool the base of the pot in a little ice water.

FOR THE SAUTÉED PEAS: Sauté the chopped onion in oil. Add the peas and cook slowly until the peas are tender. Season to taste.

PRESENTATION: Spoon a little cream of asparagus into a bowl and spoon a tablespoon of peas into it.

Cold blood sausage with cabbage and apple puree

INGREDIENTS (FOR 12 PINTXOS):

2 blood sausages (black puddings) from Beasain
1 onion
1 egg
1 sharp cooking apple
Olive oil
Butter
Sliced bread

FOR THE CABBAGE PURÉE:

½ cabbage
2 cloves garlic
1 potato

Bake the blood sausage at 190° C for 20 minutes to get rid of the fat. While the sausage is cooking, peel the apple and dice it. Sauté the cubes in a little butter and set aside.

Sauté the onion in olive oil. When golden, remove the skin from the sausage and sauté the sausagemeat and onions together. When cooked, blend in a food processor and strain through a fine sieve. Add the diced apple to the resulting cream, mix well, add an egg, mix well again and spoon the mixture into a piping bag.

FOR THE CABBAGE PURÉE: Cook the potato with the cabbage for about half an hour.

While the potato and cabbage are cooking, slice the garlic and fry it in olive oil.

Once the potato and cabbage are cooked, add the sautéed garlic and blend in a food processor until creamy.

PRESENTATION: Cut slices of bread, place a few spoonfuls of the sausage and onion mix on them and roll them up.

Fry the rolled sandwiches in the fryer carefully so they do not open.

Present them in a bowl or dish, putting a little cabbage cream at the bottom and the blood sausage roll on top.

Zeruko

Pescadería, 10. Old Quarter. Tel. 943 42 34 51

OPENED IN 1982

Zeruko is the bar that has made the most radical change from its beginnings to the current day. In 1982, Felix Calvo sold his boat, the 'Zeruko ama' (*Heavenly mother*), and took up the helm at the Zeruko bar. The Zeruko then went from being a traditional bar where pintxos and portions were served to being the leading exponent of modernity and Ferran Adriá's cuisine in the Old Quarter. His son, Joxean Calvo, makes pintxos that are a marvel of colour, smell and flavour and have won him numerous awards, including the Golden Plate at the Gipuzkoa Championship 2010 with 'Bob Limón', or second place in 2015 with 'Black Tripe'. Recently, a new Zeruko has opened its doors in Barcelona, taking the concepts of this essential bar to the Mediterranean.

Broken mussel

INGREDIENTS (MAKES 12 PINTXOS):
200 g dried ground mussel meat

FOR THE MUSSEL DOUGH: 1 onion • 1 clove garlic • 1 green pepper • 6 piquillo peppers • 50 g green olives 30 g tuna in oil • 100 g flour • Olive oil • 1litre milk

FOR THE MUSSEL SHELL: 120 g lard • Powdered squid ink • Breadcrumbs

FOR THE TOMATO SPHERE: Tomato • Tabasco • Perrin's sauce • 6 g Gluco gelling agent

FOR THE BASE: 200 g mushrooms • Garlic • White wine • Black pepper • Salt

FOR THE MUSSEL SHELL: Cut 10 x 12 g pieces of lard and mix them together with 100 g dried ground mussels (set aside the other 100 g). Coat them in the powdered squid ink and breadcrumbs and fry them, making a hole, so that the lard melts out and you are left with the half-empty shell.

FOR THE MUSSEL DOUGH: Sauté diced onion, garlic and green pepper. Add the remaining 100 g mussels, with the flour and milk, to make a béchamel sauce. Once the sauce is made, add the olives, tuna and piquillo peppers, all finely chopped. Blend in a food processor and divide the resulting mass in two; make half of it more liquid by adding water and put it in a syphon, and set aside the other half.

FOR THE TOMATO SPHERE: Using the Gluco gelling agent, make a sphere with Tabasco and Perrin's Sauce.

FOR THE BASE OF THE PINTXO: Dice the mushrooms and cook them with garlic and white wine. Let them reduce gradually, as if making a risotto.

PRESENTATION: Make a small island with the stewed mushrooms in the middle of the plate. Put the mussel shell on it, and the mussel dough next to it, as if the mussel had come out of the shell. Next to this, place the tomato sphere and spray the whole pintxo with the mixture in the syphon.

Tolosa Sashimi

Eusko Label prize in the Euskal Herria Pintxo Championship, 2015

INGREDIENTS (MAKES 10 PINTXOS):
1 kg T-bone steak from Alejandro Goya
Aioli made from black garlic
Olive oil
100 g of small green peppers
Beef fat (for carbonising)
Squid ink powder
Red and green shiso flowers
Sesame

FOR THE BISCUIT:
50 g white bread
6 g tempura flour
50 ml water
Salt
Sweet paprika
50 g beef fat
10 g of squid ink powder

Dissect the chop and divide it into three pieces; each will have to make ten slices, as each pintxo has three slices. Leave one piece, the thinnest, to marinate with salt and sugar in equal proportions for 30 hours.

Sear a second piece for a few seconds on a hot griddle and then marinate in cider and soy for the same length of time, to serve as tataki.

Try to roll the third piece, the largest, into as tight a cylindrical roll as possible, which will be called the 'carbonised meat'; coat it in the toasted grease and squid powder. Then make it into a roll, like a salami, using cling film to hold it in place.

Cook the peppers and blend them in a food processor to a thin cream.

FOR THE BISCUIT: Mix the ingredients and grind them slowly in the blender until mixed to a dough. Spoon the mixture into a piping bag. Prepare a baking sheet with baking paper, press out 10 thin biscuits and bake them for 20 minutes at 130° C until they are crisp.

PRESENTATION: Spread a little black garlic aioli onto a crisp biscuit and add the three textures of meat: first, cut a slice of the piece marinated with salt and sugar very thinly, like ham, and put it, rolled up, on one edge of the biscuit.

In the centre, place a slice of the piece of the meat prepared as tataki, and sprinkle it with a few sesame seeds.

Finally, take the 'carbonised' roll, sear it on a hot griddle with smoked salt until it is toasted, cover it with salt and squid powder, cut a slice that is thicker than the others and place it on the opposite edge of the biscuit. Spread some piquillo pepper cream on it.

Sprinkle the shiso flowers over the three pieces of meat and serve the pintxo on a stone with a little hole with a piece of burning coal so that the T-bone pintxo appears in the midst of smoke, reminiscent of the fabulous grill restaurants in Tolosa.

Bob limón

Golden Plate in the Pintxo Championship of Gipuzkoa, 2010

INGREDIENTS (MAKES 30 PINTXOS):

FOR THE CAKE:
Zest of 5 lemons
150 g ground almonds
150 g sugar
50 g dehydrated yogurt
1 litre pasteurized egg white

FOR THE FALSE FRIED EGG WHITE:
2 litres milk
200 g concentrated lemon juice

FOR THE FALSE FRIED EGG YOLK:
½ litre passion fruit syrup
Gluco (gelling agent)

FOR THE FALSE SAUSAGE:
100 g freeze-dried berries
100 g sugar
100 g ground almonds
20 g butter
A Szechuan button flower

FOR THE CAKE: Grate the 5 lemons and mix the lemon rind with the sugar, ground almonds, yogurt and egg whites. Mix in a blender.

Strain the mixture and spoon it into 2 siphons with 2 cartridges each.

Distribute the mixture, with the aid of the siphon, into small plastic cups; put two fingers' depth into each cup.

Put each cup into the microwave for 15 seconds at full power.

Remove the cake from the cups.

FOR THE FALSE FRIED EGG WHITE: Mix the milk with the concentrated lemon juice, mix well with the blender until you get a thick lemon mousse.

FOR THE FALSE FRIED EGG YOLK: Mix the passion fruit syrup with Gluco gelling agent and make 5 g spheres.

FOR THE FALSE SAUSAGE: Mix all the ingredients to make a dough and shape it like a sausage. Wrap it in cling film and let it dry out in the oven for 5 or 6 hours, so that it is hard on the outside.

PRESENTATION: Put the cake upright on one side of the plate, like bread. Place the lemon mousse in the centre and place the passion fruit sphere on top, to look like a fried egg. Finally, next to the egg, the roll of false sausage. The pintxo looks like a fried egg with bread and sausage, but it is in fact a dessert.

Black tripe

Silver Plate in the Pintxo Championship of Gipuzkoa, 2015

INGREDIENTS (MAKES 20 PINTXOS):
1 kg cod tripe
100 g tomato sauce
50 g squid ink
7 cloves garlic
1 Zopako bread
Chicken stock
Dried red chorizo pepper
0.4° C Olive oil

DECORATION:
Leeks
Fresh chives
Seasonal edible flowers

Cook the cod tripe for 10 minutes. Remove from the water and clean the tripe thoroughly. Once clean, put back in the water and cook again for two hours.

Once cooked, chop into small cubes like grains of rice. Cook à la pil-pil with a clove of garlic and a little olive oil, moving the pan gently until the gelatine from the cod thickens into a sauce. Then add the tomato sauce and squid ink.

Evaporate the sauce for half an hour on a low heat. Cool the reduced sauce and roll it into a sausage shape using cling film. Set aside.

Make a traditional garlic soup with 6 cloves of garlic, Zopako bread and chicken stock. Blend in a food processor to a creamy consistency. Set aside.

Finely chop the leek and set aside.

PRESENTATION: Cut a 5cm piece of the sausage shape and grill on a hot griddle on both sides. Dip it in the garlic soup cream.

Place the fried leek and edible flowers on top, creating a kind of crown.

Garnish with freshly chopped chives.

Rosagante (Lobster + Rose)

INGREDIENTS (MAKES 12 PINTXOS):
1 kg strawberries
6 wafers of Moroccan pasta
120 g lobster legs
Olive oil
Maldon salt
Aioli
Elixir of roses
Grenadine syrup
60 g dry ice
Green cocoa butter spray

Blend the strawberries in a food processor and spread the resulting pulp out on a sheet of baking paper. Dry the strawberry purée for at least 4 hours, so that it is very thin, like a sheet. Cut the sheet into pieces and put them into circular moulds to make the shape of a rosebud.

Cut the wafers of Moroccan pasta into the shape of rose leaves and fry them in olive oil. Once fried, spray-paint them with green cocoa butter.

Remove the meat from the lobster legs, blend in a food processor and shape into 10 g burgers. Cook on a hot griddle with salt and oil.

PRESENTATION: Prepare a glass, put some dry ice into it and cover it with the elixir of roses.

Assemble the rose by first placing the pasta leaf, then the rosebud made from strawberries, and on the rose, the lobster burger topped with a little aioli.

Thread the rose onto a long stick that will act as the stem and put it in the glass before serving the pintxo.

A Fuego Negro

31 de Agosto, 31. Old Quarter. Tel. 650 13 53 73

OPENED IN 2006

"Eat, drink, listen, watch ...and learn!" is the battle cry of this small, elegant, ground-breaking bar, since its diabolical opening on 6-6-06. Informality, experimentation, fresh ideas and a passion for hip-hop music are the hallmarks of this unusual bar run by Edorta Lamo and Amaia García and it also works as a culture lab, with exhibitions, comic books, plays, videos, music and recipes. AFN's enthusiasm is infectious and they have managed to involve people like Xabier Gutierrez, Juan Mari Arzak, Fermín Muguruza, Axel Casas or Ronkete in their projects. It is a bar like La Cuchara, whose model has been copied ad nauseam, , although no other bar has come even close to the original.

Grilled octopus, green apple, purple potato and red froth

INGREDIENTS:
1 octopus (4-5 kg)
Purple potato
Green apple
Smoked olive oil

FOR THE RED FROTH:
1 litre water
20 g sweet paprika
2 tablespoons soy lecithin

COOKING THE OCTOPUS: Wash the octopus. First, scald it by dipping it in a pan of boiling water 3-4 times, and then boil the water again and cook the octopus for about 25 minutes. Turn off the heat, cover the pan completely with cling film and leave it to finish cooking for about 20-25 minutes. Drain the octopus and let it cool.

FOR THE PURPLE POTATO: Roast the potatoes in the oven at 180° C. Peel and mash the potatoes. Add a splash of smoked oil and salt and stir to get a rough mashed texture.

FOR THE RED FROTH: Pour 20 g paprika, a little salt and two tablespoons of soy lecithin into one litre of water. Beat with a stick blender and emulsify to a froth.

PRESENTATION: Cut a slice of about 2 cm from the thickest part of the octopus tentacle. Cut in half and fry in a non-stick pan over a high heat with a little smoked oil. When browned, place each half on two walls of a rectangular mould. Fill the rest of the mould with the mashed potatoes and press. Cut a very thin slice of green apple, fold it like a handkerchief and press it into the mashed potato. On top, place a quenelle of the paprika froth.

Brava potato skins

INGREDIENTS:

3 kg potatoes

FOR THE SALSA BRAVA HOT SAUCE:

5 litre mixed meat stock
200 g garlic
1500 g onion
7.5 g paprika
500 g homemade tomato sauce
200 g vinegar reduced to 50 g
40 g salt
5 g xanthan gum
50 g potato starch

Peel the potatoes to get thin strips of peel. Wash the strips in cold water, stirring them and changing the water 10 times. Keep them in plenty of water in the fridge for 48 hours, changing the water every 12 hours.

Sauté the skins in plenty of olive oil at about 120° C until soft. Drain and fry them in plenty of olive oil to about 200° C, stirring them and frying them completely. Drain onto a tray with kitchen tissue and salt them.

FOR THE SALSA BRAVA: Sauté garlic and onion, finely diced. Once sautéed, add the paprika, chillies and then the tomato and reduced vinegar. Cook everything until soft and then add the stock. Cook for 10 minutes, strain and cool. When cold, put the sauce in the Thermomix appliance, add the xanthan gum and starch and boil. Set aside.

PRESENTATION: When serving, fill a small plate with potato skins and place a mini sauce bottle with *salsa brava* sauce on the side so that the diner can add sauce to taste.

A FUEGO NEGRO
TATAU BISTRO

Mackerel, cherries, lamb and mint

INGREDIENTS:

FOR THE CHERRY TOAST:
200 g puréed cherries
50 g powdered egg white
25 g caster sugar
25 g maltodextrin

FOR THE SHEEP CHEESE:
800 g sheep cheese
200 ml cream
3.6 g tapioca
Salt

FOR THE MARINATED MACKEREL:
12 mackerel (approx. 600g each)
1 kg sugar
1 kg coarse salt
Smoked unfiltered extra virgin olive oil (Hojiblanca)
Fresh mint
Basil sprouts
Red lettuce
Mizuna (Japanese greens)

FOR THE CHERRY TOAST: Make a cherry meringue, beating the cherry purée and powdered egg white. As the eggs start to form peaks, add the sugar and maltodextrin slowly.

Spread the meringue mixture out with a spatula onto baking paper, 1-2 cm deep. Put into a dehydrator or oven and dry at 60° C.

FOR THE SHEEP CHEESE: Using a Thermomix appliance, mix the sheep's cream cheese with the cream and tapioca. Add a pinch of salt and raise the temperature to 100° C, beating at top speed. After reaching this temperature, pour the cream into a tray to a height of about 5 cm. Cool in the fridge.

FOR THE MARINATED MACKEREL: Fillet the mackerel removing all the skin and bones. Mix the salt and sugar. Place the mackerel fillets on a tray, completely covering them with the salt/sugar mixture and leave at room temperature for 2 hours. Then wash the fillets carefully, dry them and cover them with olive oil.

PRESENTATION: Cut small cubes of mackerel and mix them with a little freshly chopped mint. Cut similar sized cubes of the cheese mix, add to the mackerel and place them carefully a piece of cherry toast.. Garnish with some basil sprouts and a sprig of fresh mizuna and red lettuce.

Prawn, egg & mayonnaise revival

INGREDIENTS:
10 fresh Huelva prawns
French bread
1 tbsp. homemade barbecue sauce
10 quail eggs

FOR THE MAYONNAISE:
80 g pasteurized egg yolk
80 g milk
340 g sunflower oil
80 g Arbequina olive oil
50 g cream
10 g lemon
6 g salt

FOR THE STICKS:
300g Mannitol
30 g icing sugar
Silicone stick mould

Blanch the prawns in boiling seawater and cool them in iced water. Set aside, reserving the heads and discarding the rest of the shell except for the tip of the tail.

Sauté the heads in a hot frying pan, add barbecue sauce and cover with iced water. Crush the heads with the back of a wooden spoon and then cook them over a low heat for two hours. Remove from the heat and leave to infuse in the pan, covered with cling film until cool. Strain the stock and set aside.

Cut half a baguette of frozen bread into slices ½ cm thick in a meat slicer. Place them on a baking tray on greaseproof paper and pour the prawn-head juice over them. Bake at 50° C until dry, crush them and set aside.

Cut the other half of the frozen baguette into slices 1 cm thick, remove the crust with a circular cutter and fry in olive oil at about 150° C. Set aside.

Cook the eggs in salted water, boiling for two minutes, stirring them slightly with a slotted spoon. Cool them in ice water, peel them and put them into a bowl of brine made with 10g of salt per litre of water.

FOR THE MAYONNAISE: Beat the egg yolks with the milk and add the oils gradually until they emulsify. Finally add the lemon juice, salt and cream. Strain, put in a syphon with two cartridges and leave in the fridge.

FOR THE STICKS: Mix the sugars well and heat them in a saucepan over a low heat until they start to turn slightly brown. Pour them carefully into the silicone moulds shaped like sticks. Cool and press out the moulds carefully. Set aside.

PRESENTATION: Press a stick carefully through the middle of the fried bread. Very carefully, stick the egg and the prawn covered with the prawn crumbs onto the vertical stick. Place in a bowl on a base of mayonnaise foam and garnish with a parsley leaf.

Cool Marianito vermouth (Marianito fresh!)

INGREDIENTS:
For osmosised orange:
2 oranges
300 ml *The Beltza* vermouth

FOR THE VERMOUTH GRANITA:
1 litre *The Beltza* vermouth
1 sheet gelatine

FOR SWEET OLIVES:
10 large pitted olives
100 ml olive juice
100 g sugar

FOR FINAL PRESENTATION:
Fennel flower

FOR THE OSMOSISED ORANGE: Peel the oranges with a sharp knife. Place the peeled orange segments on a tray with the vermouth and seal them in a vacuum pack. Put in the fridge for a minimum of two hours.

Open the bag and remove the orange segments. Place them in the orange juice.

FOR THE VERMOUTH GRANITA: Reduce the vermouth to half by boiling it, take off the heat and add the soaked gelatine. Freeze.

FOR THE SWEET OLIVES: Make a TPT syrup with the juice and sugar. Once cool, vacuum-pack the syrup along with the olives, sliced fairly thick. Set aside.

PRESENTATION: When serving, first cool a glass dish in the freezer. Scrape some vermouth granita with a fork and put a tablespoon of the scrapings at the bottom of the dish. Place three osmosised orange segments on top and next to them, three slices of sweet olives. Garnish with a fennel flower.

This recipe is a tribute to one of the concoctions par excellence of the bars here, "the Marianito", a vermouth aperitif. Our passion for the philosophy of bars is such that we have produced our own vermouth, The Beltza, we wanted to use it to make a cool, light dessert.

New arrivals

AZKENA · CASA UROLA · ZAZPI KATA 4 · ELOSTA

After the creative and conceptual boom of the first decade of the twenty-first century, there have been a few years of stagnation, coinciding with the economic crisis we have not yet emerged from. Areas which in the glorious years (2001-2006) saw spectacular growth, such as the "Golden Mile" of Gros, suffered a clear setback at the beginning of this decade, making it clear that all that glittered was not gold. In recent years, however, these areas have begun to recover, thanks to the influence of restauranteurs who are committed to original and innovative styles and also thanks to international tourism, which, despite the crisis, has increased year after year at a breakneck speed.

The consumer has changed, as have culinary trends. Whoever goes out for pintxos wants to be pleased more

than surprised, they want the bar to have good ingredients, seasonal products, good service, wines that change and and for a reasonable price.

Although it may seem contradictory considering the above, except the last point about the price, the relatively recent introduction of another phenomenon is significant; the *pintxo-pote* (pintxo + drink), which is directly related to the economic crisis and, despite having many detractors, is vital for some establishments. The *pintxo-pote*, although created as a rather vulgar phenomenon, has evolved and today there are many bars that have given it dignity, putting variety and quality into the *pintxo-pote* like the rest of their products, even though it only takes place once a week.

Bars within markets; grill houses with seasonal pintxos; young, excited, creative chefs; oyster bars; Oriental cuisine ... this chapter, one of the most exciting and original of the whole book, contains the most modern, innovative pintxos in the city.

DON'T MISS:

ESSENCIA
Zabaleta, 42. Gros

KENJI SUSHI BAR
Mayor, 6. Old Quarter

DRINKA
Matia, 50. El Antiguo

LOBO
Jose María Sert, 10. Benta Berri

LASARTE
Avda. Barcelona, 18.
Riberas de Loiola

SENRA
San Francisco, 32. Gros

KASUAL BAR
Avda. Zurriola, 4. Gros

AIZKORRI
Usandizaga, 20. Gros

BISTROTEKA ASTORIA 7
Sagrada Familia, 1. Amara

BEHARRI SAGARDOTEGIA
Narrika, 22. Old Quarter

Azkena

Bretxa Market, nº 36. Old Quarter. Tel. 615 79 26 55
OPENED IN 2000

It is fashionable to open bars in markets; no self-respecting capital lacks a 'gastronomic market'; a tourist trap and mostly for the clueless, I'd say. However, this is not the case with the Azkena in the Bretxa Market. The market, which opened in 1870, underwent a major transformation in late 2000, but still has most of the original stalls on the ground floor. This is where Iñigo Mas and Mertxe Bengoetxea, both trained by Martín Berasategui, had the great idea of installing their bar. Since then the Azkena has become famous for Mertxe's creativity; she uses seasonal ingredients from the market itself and makes beautiful food figurines of the Guggenheim, the *Peine del Viento* statue and the Kursaal building.

Black pudding with cabbage, with mint, chocolate and red bean cream

INGREDIENTS (MAKES 6 PINTXOS):

FOR THE BLACK PUDDING AND GARNISH:
1 black pudding or blood sausage with onion
2 slices spicy chorizo (in small pieces)
½ slice pork tenderloin (in small pieces)
½ cabbage
3 cloves garlic
Olive oil
Salt

FOR THE RED BEAN CREAM:
500 g Tolosa beans
1 onion (chopped)
1 dash extra virgin olive oil

FOR THE BLACK PUDDING AND GARNISH: Remove the skin from the blood sausage and fry it in olive oil with the spicy chorizo, and pork loin. Add salt and set aside.

Chop the cabbage into strips. Wash and cook in salted water. Drain well. Sauté the garlic in olive oil and add it to the cabbage. Set aside.

FOR THE RED BEAN CREAM: Leave the red beans to soak overnight in abundant cold water. The next day, leave the beans in the water where they have been soaking, add the onion and a dash of extra virgin olive oil and bring them to the boil. Break the boil three times with a little cold water and leave the beans to simmer gently for about 2 hours. When cooked, blend in a food processor and set aside.

PRESENTATION: Put a few fried potatoes in the bottom of a bowl, and place the black pudding and cabbage on top. On top, place a few more slices of fried potato, and then add onion sauce and chocolate sauce.

Serve with Tolosa bean cream, slices of fried garlic and fresh mint.

Peine del Viento

(Veal Cheeks with twisted pasta, strawberries in red wine and vanilla froth)

INGREDIENTS (MAKES 8 PINTXOS):
4 veal cheeks
2 onions
1 leek
1 carrot
1 glass of brandy
¼ litre port
1 litre red wine
1 litre beef stock

FOR THE STRAWBERRIES IN RED WINE:
½ kg strawberries
6 tbsp. sugar
½ litre red wine
Peel of 1 orange
1 cinnamon stick

FOR THE VANILLA FROTH:
400 ml water
100 ml milk
2 vanilla pods
1.5 g soy lecithin

FOR THE VEAL CHEEKS: Sauté the vegetables. In another pan, season and sear the veal cheeks, drain the oil and flambé them with the brandy. Add the port, the red wine and the sautéed vegetables, cook well and add the stock, cooking gently until tender. Remove the meat from the pan. Reduce the sauce until it is a quarter of the initial volume, return the cheeks in slices to the sauce and cook them slowly until they are glazed.

FOR THE STRAWBERRIES: Cut the strawberries in half. Heat the red wine in a saucepan with the sugar, cinnamon and orange. Cook for 20 minutes, add the strawberries and leave for 5 minutes more. Allow to cool.

FOR THE VANILLA FROTH: Boil the ingredients, strain and blend at high speed to get a froth.

FOR THE TWISTED PASTA: Boil water in a large pan. When boiling, put the pasta in the water and cook al dente. Cool under cold water, drain and fry to give it a twisted shape.

PRESENTATION: Use potato purée as a base. Place a few slices of veal cheek with sauce and strawberries. Decorate with the twisted pasta as if it were a 'wind comb' like the Chillida statue, with vanilla froth for the sea and some corn chips as cobblestones.

Tuna steak with squid in ink between bamboo rice and mint

INGREDIENTS (MAKES 6 PINTXOS):

FOR THE TUNA AND GARNISH:
2 slices of fresh tuna steak
Olive oil
Maldon salt
Chard stems
Cooked rice noodles

FOR THE SQUID IN INK:
16 fresh squid
½ onion
½ green pepper
½ clove garlic
4 tbsp. tomato sauce
½ glass red wine
1 dl oil
Squid ink
Salt

FOR THE TUNA AND GARNISH: Clean the tuna, removing the skin and bones. Cut into thick steaks and season. Set aside.

Brush the steaks with olive oil and sear them for a minute on each side in a very hot pan, keeping them juicy and pink inside. Set aside.

Peel the chard stems and remove any threads. Chop into rectangles and cook for 5 minutes, then dip in egg and flour and fry.

FOR THE SQUID IN INK: Clean the squid thoroughly and reserve the ink. Sauté the onion, green pepper, garlic and salt. Cut the squid into small pieces and sauté in olive oil in a hot pan. Season and set aside.

Add the squid to the sautéed vegetables, with the tomato sauce and red wine. Simmer gently for a few minutes and add the ink with a little water or stock. Cook slowly for a while. Remove the squid, strain or blend the sauce, return the squid to the pan and add salt.

PRESENTATION: Place a rectangle of chard on a slate and the squid, a piece of tuna and another chard stem on top. Pour the sauce over the pintxo. Serve with fried pasta shaped like bamboo, fresh mint and liqueur foam.

Warm salad of vegetables with octopus and sweet paprika

INGREDIENTS (MAKES 6 PINTXOS):

FOR THE VEGETABLES:
100 g green beans
50 g cauliflower
250 g cabbage
1 clove garlic
Mild paprika
Olive oil
Balsamic vinegar
Salt

FOR THE OCTOPUS:
2 cooked octopus legs
Salt

FOR THE OCTOPUS: Clean the octopus and cook in salted water. Blanch it 3 times in boiling water for a few seconds and then cook it for 40 minutes. Once cooled, remove the legs and cut them into slices.

FOR THE VEGETABLES: Boil the green beans and cauliflower in salted water. Set aside. Cut the cabbage into julienne strips and dress it with a little oil and sliced garlic. Add the green beans and cauliflower, and sauté with the sliced garlic.

PRESENTATION: Place a few slices of fried potato on a plate. Arrange the sautéed vegetables and sliced octopus on top. Season with olive oil, balsamic vinegar and coarse salt. Serve with white onion sauce, mild paprika and crispy rice paper.

Squid omelette with tentacles

INGREDIENTS (MAKES 6 PINTXOS):

250 g of small squid
½ onion, chopped
1 clove garlic, chopped
½ green pepper, chopped
Fish stock or water
8 eggs
Olive oil
Salt

Clean the squid and remove the innards. Peel the skin off and cut the squid into small pieces. Separate the tentacles and set aside. Fry the squid pieces in hot oil, season and cook until the liquid evaporates. Add a tablespoon of oil, onion, garlic, green pepper and leave to sauté. Moisten with half the stock, boil and add beaten eggs. Season.

Cook the omelette until it sets, turning half-way through cooking and ensuring that it doesn't dry out.

Fry the squid tentacles with cornflour, salt and oil.

PRESENTATION: Place the squid omelette on a round plate. On top, accompany each serving or pintxo with slices of crispy cheese, fried rice noodles, the squid tentacles and black ink sauce.

Casa Urola

Fermín Calbetón, 20. Old Quarter. Tel. 943 44 13 71

OPENED IN 1948. RECENTLY REOPENED IN 2013

The Urola remains one of the great classics of the Old Quarter. After its closure in 2011, announced with a lot of fuss, everyone thought it had gone for ever, but in 2013 it was taken on by Pablo Loureiro, a chef obsessed with seasonal produce; besides triumphantly reopening the restaurant, he has moved his passion for fresh cuisine to making pintxos. Thus, on the changing, ever-dynamic menu slate of the Urola, we find game and mushrooms in autumn and winter, artichokes and asparagus in spring and green beans in summer. It is a display of seasonal produce, impeccably presented and prepared with great technical ability, which shows the long, intense career of this chef; he is apparently quiet and timid, but has a playful, mischievous soul.

Sautéed green beans with tomatoes, pine nuts, potato foam and black olive oil

INGREDIENTS (MAKES 4 PINTXOS):

400 g green beans
40 g pine nuts
60 g chopped tomatoes
30 g Iberian ham, finely chopped
200 g salt cod
1 dl olive oil macerated with garlic and green chilli pepper

FOR THE BLACK OLIVE OIL:

20 black olives
150 g Arbequina extra virgin olive oil

FOR THE POTATO FOAM:

300 g cooked potato
100 g cream
50 g Arbequina olive oil
100 g cooking water from the potatoes
Salt

Cut into the green beans into thin sticks, cook them in unsalted boiling water for about 4 minutes approximately. Cool them in cold water with ice cubes and set aside.

FOR THE POTATO FOAM: Blend the potatoes, cooking water, cream, salt and oil in a food processor. Allow to cool and spoon into a food syphon.

FOR THE BLACK OLIVE OIL: Remove the stone from the olives, blend them with the oil and season.

FOR THE COD CONFIT: Confit the cod by immersing it in a container with the garlic and chilli oil and putting it in the microwave 3 times for about 30 seconds each at full power.

PRESENTATION: Sauté the beans with the diced tomatoes and pine nuts. Remove from the heat and add the chopped ham. Arrange on the plate by making a volcano with beans and flakes of cod confit. Inside the volcano add the potato foam and finally a trickle of black olive oil. Decorate with sticks of fried bread, slices of ham or bean sprouts.

Octopus and pork jowl brochette, potato and garlic soup, paprika oil and sautéed cabbage

INGREDIENTS (MAKES 4 PINTXOS):

FOR THE BROCHETTE:
8 thick slices of octopus
8 thin slices of Iberian pork jowl
4 x 15cm skewers

FOR THE POTATO AND GARLIC SOUP:
150 g cooked potato
225 g potato cooking water
1 dl mild olive oil
2 cloves garlic
Salt

FOR THE PAPRIKA OIL:
1 dl garlic confit oil
10 g mild paprika
Salt

FOR THE FRIED BREADCRUMBS:
25 g *panko* (Japanese breadcrumbs)
1 dl garlic oil

FOR THE SAUTÉED CABBAGE:
2 cabbage leaves with stalks removed
Garlic oil
Salt

OPTIONAL:
4 sprigs of rosemary or sage, salt flakes

FOR THE BROCHETTES: Thread the skewers with 2 slices of octopus and 2 slices of pork jowl, alternating.

FOR THE POTATO AND GARLIC SOUP: Mash the potatoes with hot cooking water and at the end, add olive oil that has been confited with garlic (remove the garlic before adding the oil to the mix). Add salt and strain.

FOR THE PAPRIKA OIL: Blend the oil with the paprika and add salt.

FOR THE FRIED BREADCRUMBS: Fry the *panko* in garlic oil until golden brown. Drain and dry on kitchen paper to remove excess oil.

FOR THE SAUTÉED CABBAGE: Cut two cabbage leaves into thin julienne strips and stir fry them raw with a little oil and salt. Cover them to sweat, taking care not to burn them. They should still have a crunchy texture.

PRESENTATION: Place the sautéed cabbage at the bottom of four bowls. Drizzle them with the potato and garlic soup and draw lines with the paprika oil. Sear the octopus brochettes in a pan or on the griddle on both sides and place one in each bowl. Add some salt flakes, the fried *panko* and a sprig of rosemary or sage.

Grilled artichoke and thistle, cream of ham and salted almond praline

INGREDIENTS (MAKES 4 PINTXOS):
6 artichokes
4 stalks of thistle 5 cm. long
Mild olive oil
Water
Salt
Parsley stalks
6 slices of Iberian ham
Ground almonds
Extra virgin olive oil (if possible, the brand Koroneiki)

FOR THE CREAM OF HAM:
200 g tips and stems of the cooked artichokes
70 g olive oil garlic confit
The end piece of a cured ham
100 g ham broth

FOR SALTED ALMOND PRALINE:
100 g toasted almonds
30 g sunflower oil
Salt flakes

Clean the artichokes, saving part of the stems and outside leaves for the cream of ham. Plunge all parts of the artichokes into cold water with the parsley stems, so they do not go black. Steam them with a splash of mild olive oil and a pinch of salt until tender or boil them in water with a little oil, salt and parsley stalks for 5 minutes and let them cool completely in the water.

Clean the thistle stems like the artichokes, steaming until tender or boiling them in water with salt and olive oil for 30 - 40 minutes.

FOR THE CREAM OF HAM: Blend the tips and stems of artichokes, confit oil and ham broth in a food processer. Press through a sieve to remove any woody fibres from the cream.

FOR SALTED ALMOND PRALINE: Blend toasted almond, sunflower oil and salt in a food processor and strain.

PRESENTATION: Cut the artichokes in half and sear them on a hot griddle. Sear the thistle too and set aside.

Assemble on a plate by first making a circle with the almond praline. In the centre, spoon the hot cream of ham. On this, place three half artichokes and a stalk of thistle with a drizzle of extra virgin olive oil. Top it with slices of ham and sprinkle with ground almonds.

Spring salad

INGREDIENTS (MAKES 4 PINTXOS):
150 g mixed lettuce leaves
60 g young broad beans, peeled
40 g toasted pine nuts
80 g foie gras
6 chopped cooked prawns
1 handful St George's mushrooms
12 chive flowers

FOR THE COFFEE VINAIGRETTE:
½ an espresso coffee
4 dl sunflower oil
Salt
White pepper

Make the coffee vinaigrette by mixing the four ingredients in a blender until homogenised. Set aside.

PRESENTATION: Arrange the mixed lettuce leaves as the base of the pintxo. Cut the foie gras into small cubes and place it on the lettuce base, followed by the young beans, pine nuts and chopped prawns.

Dress with the coffee vinaigrette, and add the raw mushroom in slices. Add some more dressing and garnish with 3 chive flowers.

Roasted mushroom cap with pine nuts and egg yolk

INGREDIENTS (MAKES 8 PINTXOS):
8 or 16 small mushrooms (depending on size)
2 dl olive oil confit with 4 cloves garlic
1 tablespoon toasted pine nuts
8 egg yolks
2 dl duck gravy (made with duck carcasses, vegetables, chickpeas, herbs, brandy, mushrooms and black pepper)
1 sprig rosemary

FOR THE POTATO FOAM:
350 g cooked potato
125g potato cooking water
125 g cream
65 g of Arbequina olive oil
Salt

FOR THE MUSHROOMS: Wash them and cut half the stem off, to be chopped with the toasted pine nuts. Place the mushroom caps with the garlic oil and salt in a vacuum bag and cook them sous vide in a Roner appliance at 85º C for about 20 minutes.

FOR THE POTATO FOAM: Blend all the ingredients in a food processor, strain and spoon the mix into a food siphon with one cartridge. Set aside.

PRESENTATION: Heat the mushroom caps quickly in a hot oven, drizzle the duck gravy on the plate, pile up the chopped mushroom and the toasted pine nuts like a volcano on one side of the plate, heat the egg yolk under a high temperature grill or poach it and place it on top. On the other side of the plate, place the mushroom caps and in the middle of the plate, the warm potato foam.

Finally, garnish with a sprig of rosemary and a few flakes of salt.

Elosta

Paseo de Colón, 41. Gros. Tel. 843 63 03 25

REOPENED IN 2013

Mikel Lopez was a bad student but ended up as a cook, and got his first job in the Atalaia of Inaxio Muguruza. Since then, this young man from San Sebastián has embarked on a long journey which has included the Akelarre and the Kokotxa, restaurants of great prestige run by his brother Dani, and places as varied as the Val d'Aran, the Ibiza and the Lanzarote, before finally setting up this unusual bar-restaurant. He defines it as "just a restaurant with good food", but Mikel makes Japanese food with Peruvian touches and Basque influence. It makes for a highly original cocktail, especially considering that all the staff are Western and that Mikel has never travelled (not yet, at any rate) to Japan or Peru.

Salmon tartare

INGREDIENTS:

40 g of salmon
1/6 of an avocado
Hydrated wakame seaweed
Chives
Salt
Black tobiko (flying fish roe)
Japanese mayonnaise
Bean sprouts
Toasted bread

Chop the salmon, avocado and seaweed and mix with the mayonnaise, chives and salt.

Place a quenelle of this mixture on a small dish using two dessert spoons to shape it. On top, place half a teaspoon of tobiko and a few bean sprouts, and accompany it with a slice of toasted bread.

Peruvian Causa topped with crab

INGREDIENTS:

2 large potatoes
Yellow chilli pepper
Juice of half a lime
Salt
50 g flaked crab
Japanese mayonnaise
Aioli with squid ink
Flour
Egg
Breadcrumbs
Sunflower oil
Chives
Avocado cream

Boil the potatoes whole. Open the chilli peppers and remove the seeds. Boil the chilli peppers until the skin loosens, then take them out of the water, peel them and grind them with a little mild olive oil. Strain and reserve.

Peel the potatoes. Mash them roughly with a stick blender and season them with the chilli pepper paste, lime juice and salt.

Form balls as if they were croquettes and let them cool. When they are cold, roll them in flour, egg and breadcrumbs and fry them until golden brown.

Mix the crab with a little mayonnaise and spoon it and on top of the causa croquettes, garnishing them with a dot of squid ink aioli and a few chopped chives.

PRESENTATION: Put some avocado cream on a plate and top, place the causa croquette. Dab a little chilli pepper paste onto the dish.

Tuna tataki with ajoblanco soup

INGREDIENTS:
Bean sprouts
Chopped chives
Ito togarashi (dried red chilli pepper)
Plantain chips
Sesame seeds
Maldon salt
Extra virgin olive oil

FOR THE TATAKI:
Tuna
2 g of ginger
500 ml of soy sauce
2 g of garlic

FOR THE AJOBLANCO SOUP:
100 g of ground almonds
2 cloves garlic
1 litre of cold water
150 g breadcrumbs
100 ml extra virgin olive oil
30 ml sherry vinegar
A pinch of salt

FOR THE TATAKI: Grate the garlic and ginger and mix it with the soy sauce. Sear the tuna in a very hot pan for 3 seconds on each side. Put it in the marinade of garlic, ginger and soy and let it stand in the fridge for 24 hours. Remove, dry and set aside.

FOR THE AJOBLANCO SOUP: In a blender, put all the ingredients except the oil. Blend well and add the oil. Strain and put in the fridge.

FOR THE PLANTAIN CHIPS: Cut the very cold plantains and fry them in hot oil.

PRESENTATION: Put the tuna in the middle of a deep dish and surround it with the ajoblanco soup. Sprinkle with some chives, Maldon salt and sesame seeds. Put the banana chips, ito togarashi, and finish with a drizzle of extra virgin olive oil.

Seaweed salad with marinated cucumber

INGREDIENTS (MAKES 10 PINCHOS):

FOR THE ALGAE:
20 g wakame seaweed
5 g of agar
3 tablespoons rice vinegar
1 tablespoon soy sauce
1/8 chopped Thai chilli
1 teaspoon sesame oil
½ tablespoon agave syrup

FOR CUCUMBER:
1 cucumber
200 g rice vinegar
200 g water
40 g sugar
10 g salt

Soak the algae and mix them with the other ingredients

Cut the cucumber into thin slices and marinate them with the remaining ingredients. Leave in the fridge for 24 hours.

PRESENTATION: Put some seaweed and a little of the cucumber in a deep bowl. Garnish with a little sesame oil and sesame seeds.

Mini tuna burger

INGREDIENTS (MAKES 4 PINCHOS):
For the burger:
200 g of tuna
1 poached onion
Breadcrumbs in milk
1 egg
Salt
Chives
Pepper

FOR THE CREAM OF ONION:
3 onions
Olive oil
Salt

FOR THE TOMATO CONFIT:
2 tomatoes
Brown sugar
Rosemary

ALSO:
Chips, mini burger bread, rocket leaves

Chop the tuna and mix with the remaining ingredients. Mix well and form two 40g burgers.

FOR THE CREAM OF ONION: Chop onion and fry until brown, in a covered pan and over a very low heat. Blend to a paste, strain and add a pinch of salt.

FOR THE TOMATO CONFIT: Cut the tomatoes into petals and put them on a baking tray. Sprinkle them with sugar and rosemary and bake at 135° C for 40 minutes.

FOR THE CHIPS: Peel and slice the potatoes thinly. Fry in hot oil.

PRESENTATION: Fry the burger in a pan. Put it on the bread, add a little cream of onion, a baked tomato and rocket. Cover the burger with the bun and accompany with chips.

Kata 4

Santa Catalina, 4. Centre. Tel. 943 42 32 43

OPENED IN 2011

Kata 4 is the first Oyster Bar that has been successful in San Sebastián, and Ismael Iglesias is the first and youngest man from Toledo to emerge as a chef in the city, after training in the Irizar School and demonstrating his culinary skills in restaurants like Branka, Narru, Juanito Kojua, Urepel, Beti Jai or Alameda. Simply because of this impressive list, it is worth visiting this beautiful bar, where you can taste up to 7 types of oysters brought in freshly twice a week and enjoy Ismael's cooking, based on traditional cuisine, with its creative, evocative and colourful dishes. And when it comes down to it, he can also cook traditional tripe to die for. Just try it.

Tomato and tuna tartare with finger lime and fruit carpaccio

INGREDIENTS:

FOR THE TARTARE:
100g of tuna
50 g of tomato
20 g diced spring onion
Whole-grain mustard
Salt
Extra virgin Arbequina olive oil

FOR THE CARPACCIO:
2 slices pineapple
2 slices beetroot
2 slices plum
2 slices mango

TO GARNISH:
Bean sprouts
Finger lime

FOR THE TARTARE: Peel the tomatoes, remove the seeds and dice very small. Cut the tuna into small cubes and mix with the onion, mustard and salt. Season with Arbequina oil to taste.

FOR THE CARPACCIO: Cut all the fruit slices to 0.5 mm in a meat slicer.

PRESENTATION: Put four slices of carpaccio on a plate. Press the tartare into a mould and then turn it out on top of the carpaccio. Top it off with some bean sprouts and finger lime.

Squid with cauliflower purée and flame-roasted spring onion consommé

INGREDIENTS:
1 large squid
20 spring onions
1 litre white wine
1 cauliflower
Salt
Extra virgin Arbequina olive oil
Mixed baby lettuce leaves

FOR THE SPRING ONION CONSOMMÉ: Cut 20 spring onions into slices and grill them on both sides until they are burnt.

Put them into a saucepan with white wine and reduce until slightly more than half the liquid. Strain the consommé through a fine sieve with a muslin cloth.

FOR THE CAULIFLOWER PURÉE: Cook the cauliflower and blend in a food processor without water, with a little salt and Arbequina oil.

PRESENTATION: Clean the squid, leaving its skin on, and sear on a griddle or under the grill. Cut into three parts. Stand them up in a deep bowl with a few spoonfuls of cauliflower purée. Arrange the tentacles on top and garnish with baby lettuce leaves.

Serve, and pour the consommé over the dish at the table.

Roast foie gras with baby broad beans and a hint of liquorice

INGREDIENTS:
1 duck liver
Milk
Water
Salt
Sugar
Liquorice
Baby broad beans
Butter
Maldon salt

FOR THE ROASTED DUCK LIVER OR FOIE GRAS: Soak the liver in milk and water with a little salt and sugar for 12 hours. Drain and dry the liver.

Marinate the liver with a thin layer of salt and sugar (60 g of salt and 20 g of sugar per kilo of liver).

Vacuum pack the liver and cook it sous-vide in a Roner for 20 minutes at 50° C. Take it out and let it cool to room temperature. Once it has cooled, cook it again at 65° C for 30 minutes. Take it out and chill it in iced water.

Remove the liver from the vacuum bag and sear it on a hot griddle on each side.

Finally, bake the liver in the oven at 135° C for 8 to 10 minutes.

FOR THE LIQUORICE: Bake the liquorice in the oven, then steep it in boiling water. Reduce the water and blend the liquorice in a food processor to make a cream.

FOR THE BABY BROAD BEANS: Pod the beans and blanch them in boiling water for 10 - 15 seconds. Peel them and sauté them in butter.

PRESENTATION: Paint a line of liquorice cream on a plate. Place a slice of the grilled foie gras on the plate and arrange a few sautéed beans on the foie. Garnish with some flakes of Maldon salt.

Artichokes with roast scallop and shrimp consommé

INGREDIENTS (MAKES 1 PINTXO):

50 g prawns
550 ml water
1 scallop
2 artichokes
Salt

FOR THE PRAWN CONSOMMÉ: Bake the prawns at 200° C until brown. Put them to cook in ½ litre of boiling water, until the water reduces to half.

FOR THE ARTICHOKES: Clean the artichokes and boil them until they are soft. Place in a large frying pan with the consommé; bring to the boil and simmer for a few minutes. Season.

FOR SCALLOP: Sear the scallop on both sides in a hot non-stick pan.

PRESENTATION: Place the artichokes with the stems pointing upwards. Place the scallop next to them and pour the prawn consommé on top.

Crispy suckling pig's tail, potato purée and dried yogurt

INGREDIENTS:
1 pig's tail
100 g of boneless suckling pig
Pork bones
Olive oil
Water
Yogurt

FOR THE POTATO PURÉE:
Potato
Water
Extra virgin Arbequina olive oil

FOR THE PIG'S TAIL: Cook the pig's tail and suckling pig sous-vide at 90° C for 12 hours in a Roner and remove the bones. When cooked, roast or grill both cuts of meat until they become crispy.

FOR THE PORK GRAVY: Cook the pork bones from the suckling pig; sauté them in a little oil until they brown and start to burn. Add water and reduce to get a thick gravy.

FOR THE POTATO PURÉE: Cook the potatoes in water and purée them in a blender with Arbequina oil.

FOR THE DRIED YOGURT: Dry the yogurt in a dehydrator.

PRESENTATION: Spoon the purée on a plate. On top, place the boned pork, crowned with the crispy pigtail and then garnish with the dried yogurt.

Pour the gravy made from the pork bones around the dish.

Zazpi

San Marcial, 7. Centre. Tel. 943 50 67 67

REOPENED IN 2014

Veni, vidi, vinci, as the Romans said. Paul Arrillaga, not yet 30 and with an incredible CV, was looking for a place on which to unleash his creativity and the Zazpi (Seven, in Basque), located at that number in San Marcial street, had been lying vacant for a year and was looking for an owner. It was love at first sight, and he only had to open the bar, and carry the day. With the combination of Paul's culinary art and his partner Maite Mujika's knowledge of bars and restaurants, they were set for success. First thing in the morning, the Zazpi fills up with people having breakfast, then midmorning pintxos, set menus and later, evening meals. Two years later, we fear that the bar has outgrown the premises, but this is not the moment to branch out. Will this couple stay in the Zazpi? (*To be continued…*)

Pigeon breast with truffled polenta

INGREDIENTS:

Wood pigeon breasts
100 g polenta
250 g cream
250 g water
2 tsp white truffle oil
5 Granny Smith apples
100 g sugar
Wild rice
Freeze-dried raspberries
Mustard sprouts
Maldon salt
Olive oil

FOR THE POLENTA: Boil the cream with the water and truffle oil. Add the polenta and stir well. Simmer for 20 minutes, then pour the polenta into a container to form a layer 1 cm. thick and put it in the fridge. Once cool, cut a rectangle similar to the pigeon breast in length and width and set it aside.

FOR THE APPLE PURÉE: Cook the apples with sugar and a little water in a pan until they break down into purée.

PRESENTATION: Grill the pigeon breast and polenta. Fry the wild rice in plenty of oil, and assemble the dish with the pigeon breast, polenta and other ingredients to look as beautiful as possible.

Stewed pork ear

INGREDIENTS:
2 kg pig's ears
½ onion
1 carrot
1 leek
1 red pepper
100 g Iberian ham chopped into small cubes
100 g spicy chorizo chopped into small cubes
1 tsp hot paprika
1 litre tomato sauce
1.5 l cooking water from the pig's ears
2 tsp chopped chives
Olive oil

Cook the pig's ears in plenty of water for 5 hours, then drain them, reserving the cooking water.

Once cool, chop the ears into 2x2 cm cubes and set aside.

Dice the vegetables finely and fry with a little oil. After 10 minutes add the ham and chorizo and fry for 10 more minutes. Add the paprika and tomato sauce quickly. Boil everything for 5 minutes and add the pig's ear. Sauté a little and then add the cooking water. Cook for another 20 minutes approximately and check the seasoning.

PRESENTATION: Serve the stewed pig's ears in a bowl with chopped chives on top.

Beef chop with onion ashes and green peppers

INGREDIENTS:

200 g T-bone steak
50 g maltodextrin
5 g onion ashes
30g beef fat
10 green piquillo peppers
Chilli threads
Olive oil
Maldon salt

FOR THE ASHES: Mix the maltodextrin, beef fat and onion ashes together.

FOR PIQUILLO PEPPER SAUCE: Whisk the piquillo peppers in oil over a low heat for two hours and then drain them. Blend them to a smooth sauce with a stick blender.

FOR THE T-BONE STEAK: Cut a 60 g piece of beef steak approximately, and roast it on the grill or in a pan on both sides, leaving the inside rare.

PRESENTATION: Put two parallel piles of ashes on a plate. In the centre, place the portion of steak, cut in half into two triangles. On the sides, arrange the piquillo pepper sauce, then season the meat with Maldon salt and garnish it with chilli threads.

Cod with ajoarriero

INGREDIENTS:
Cod fillet
Onion sprouts

FOR THE AJOARRIERO:
Cod tripe
Onion
Red pepper
Green pepper
Chorizo meat
Tomato sauce
Olive oil

FOR THE AJOARRIERO: Dice the onion and peppers and sauté in olive oil.

Blanch the cod tripe, whole, for 2 and a half minutes in boiling water. Take it out, wait for it to cool and cut it into very small pieces, setting aside the cooking water.

Add the chopped tripe to the sautéing vegetables, cook for a while, add two tablespoons of tomato sauce and a tablespoon of chorizo meat. Let it all sauté together for a few minutes, add a litre of the tripe cooking water and let it reduce for half an hour so that the gelatine thickens it. Do not add salt.

FOR THE COD FILLET: Cook the cod fillet for 3 minutes in olive oil, skin-side up. Once cooked, drain the cod well on kitchen tissue.

PRESENTATION: In a bowl place the ajoarriero as a base. On top of it, place the well-drained cod fillet and garnish the pintxo with a handful of onion sprouts.

Sous-vide suckling pig with mole

INGREDIENTS:
¼ suckling pig
4 cloves garlic
1 lemon
Salt
Olive oil
Mole poblano
Mini Agata potatoes (boiled)
Onion sprouts
Parsley
Olive oil
Water

FOR THE SUCKLING PIG: Vacuum pack the suckling pig with garlic, lemon, oil and salt. Cook it sous-vide in the Roner for 15 hours. Let it cool, reserve the cooking juices, debone it and form a terrine putting the skin at the base of the terrine mould.

FOR THE MOLE: Add the mole paste to the juice obtained from cooking the suckling pig, to make a thick sauce.

FOR THE PARSLEY OIL: Blend the parsley with oil and water using a stick blender and then strain.

PRESENTATION: Cut a portion of suckling pig and toast it on the grill or in a pan, skin-side down.

In a shallow dish, paint a stripe of mole with a brush. On one side, place the suckling pig and on the other, the boiled potatoes with onion sprouts.

Garnish the pintxo with a few drops of parsley oil.

Hidden

MESÓN LUGARITZ · TXUBILLO ARATZ · HAIZPE · VIZCACHA

Now that we are in the twenty-first century and heading towards the final stretch of the second decade, we can say that the pintxo is a product that is here to stay. It is rare for a bar or restaurant not to offer some selection, however small, of little bites to eat, and old bars have been turned into pintxo bars; bars; pintxos have spread like wildfire from the historical centre of the city where they began and developed, to the towns and suburbs of Gipuzkoa, the Basque Country in general and beyond.

San Sebastián is no exception, and in addition to the Old Quarter, Gros and the Centre areas where most of the bars in this book are located, there are great pintxo bars in the districts of Amara, El Antiguo, Intxaurrondo, Riberas de Loiola and Egia. Also, the bars away from the tourist and business areas have

a special charm - the charm of neighbourhood bars with simpler menus - but with more authentic cuisine, more traditional... and usually cheaper. They are also bars where there is a closer, more family environment, with a regular clientele generally made up of the residents and workers from the surrounding areas.

In these bars we will not find spheres squared with Gellan, but good tripe, moist Spanish omelette, squid made in the traditional style, delicious hake between slices of bread and, if the opportunity arises, a little conversation.

It is this, no less, that we find in the five bars selected for this chapter, with the exception of Txubillo, which is a curious case of Basque-Japanese fusion, hidden in the district of El Antiguo. Also, the last two of the ten bars listed on this page, although they are in Central and Gros, are also 'hidden' bars because of their location and size; Ciaboga, famous for its potato dishes and Urkabe, celebrated for its croquettes.

DON'T MISS:

LA VENTA DE CURRO
Avenida Madrid, 32. Amara

CAFÉ S7ETE
Javier de Barkaiztegi, 13. Amara

GASTEIZ
Vitoria-Gasteiz, 12. Ondarreta

TERESATXO
Avenida Zarautz, 85. Lorea

BIGARREN
Isabel II, 6. Amara

OLIYOS
Escolta Real, 4. El Antiguo

AGUSTÍN
Sancho el Sabio, 16. Amara

IZEI
Baratzategi, 24. Intxaurrondo

CIABOGA
Easo, 9. Centre

URKABE
Segundo Izpizua, 33. Gros

Aratz

Igara Bidea, 15. Ibaeta. Tel. 943 21 92 04

OPENED IN 1989

Aratz could be defined as a neighbourhood restaurant with an international reputation. You can see students, locals, visitors from the countryside and workers from the city's offices sitting on the terrace or in the bar enjoying breakfast, a pintxo, coffee or wine. The dining room fills up with workers who come to eat their excellent set menu, and groups of friends and families are drawn here by its good fresh ingredients and excellent cooking. In the private dining room, we can see gourmets, journalists, politicians or rock stars enjoying the seasonal produce, or the spectacular range of wines. Brothers Xabier and Iker Zabaleta run a tight ship in making their customers feel good; the Aratz has sailed under them for more than 25 years and they are now cruising through the next twenty-five years on a boat that has customers and friends that admire their good food and atmosphere.

Prawn and ham brochette

INGREDIENTS (MAKES 1 PINTXO):

4 prawns
Garlic oil
1 slice of green pepper
1 slice of Iberian ham
Reduction of Modena vinegar
Chopped parsley

Grill four prawns and string them onto a skewer. Cut a large strip of green pepper and cook it at a low temperature in plenty of olive oil until it is soft.

Drizzle a plate with virgin olive oil that has been infused for several days with garlic. Place a slice of ham on the oil, and on top, the cooked slice of green pepper.

For the reduction of Modena, put 200 ml. Balsamic vinegar in a pan with 40 g of sugar. Leave it on a medium heat for about 30 minutes or until it has reduced to the desired consistency.

PRESENTATION: Put the skewered prawns on the plate with the ham and pepper and drizzle the pintxo with a few trickles of reduced balsamic vinegar. Garnish with chopped parsley.

Hidden: ARATZ

Smoked cod

INGREDIENTS (MAKES 1 PINTXO):

1 flat ice cream wafer
1 slice of homemade foie gras
1 slice of smoked cod
Cod foie
Shallot
St George's mushroom
Garlic
Oil
Sherry vinegar
Lemon
Chilli pepper
Olive oil
Parsley
Rosemary

FOR THE HOMEMADE FOIE TERRINE:

Liver
Cinnamon
Black pepper
White pepper
Black truffle in olive oil
Brandy
Maldon salt

FOR THE HOMEMADE FOIE TERRINE: Remove the veins from the liver and open it like a book. Add a large pinch of Maldon salt, black pepper, white pepper, grated truffle, and then a pinch of cinnamon and a dash of brandy.

Close the liver and place it in a rectangular tin to shape it.

Cook it in a bain-marie in the oven at 145º C for about 45 minutes.

ASSEMBLING THE PINTXO: Place the ice cream wafer as the base. On top, lay a thin slice of homemade foie gras terrine. On it, a slice of smoked cod and then, a little cod foie mixed with finely chopped shallots.

Top the pintxo with a few mushrooms broken up into pieces, either raw or lightly sautéed.

PRESENTATION: First sauté the garlic, sherry vinegar, lemon and the chilli pepper in oil until soft, and place this sauce in a food syphon.

Syphon the sauce onto the pintxo and sprinkle it with chopped parsley.

Finally, in one corner of the kitchen, place some dried rosemary on a fire-proof tray and set fire to it. Cover it with a small glass dome so that the smoke fills the dome.

Just before serving the pintxo, cover it with the dome so that the pintxo is served at the table inside the dome, enveloped in smoke.

Hidden: ARATZ

Squid in ink

INGREDIENTS:

1 large squid (1,5 - 2 kilos)
2 onions
1 carrot
1 leek
White wine
Cognac
Olive oil
Water
Salt
Croutons (optional)

FOR THE SAUCE:

Garlic
Stale bread
Olive oil
Homemade tomato sauce
Squid ink

Clean the squid and set aside the ink. Cut the cleaned squid into small squares, fry it in hot oil and then place the pieces in a casserole dish. Cover them with water and simmer with a pinch of salt.

In a separate pan, sauté the chopped onion, carrot and leek. Once the vegetables are cooked, add them to the pan where you fried the pieces of squid and flambé them with a little white wine and cognac.

In a deep saucepan, prepare the sauce; fry chopped garlic and chopped stale bread in a little olive oil. When the garlic and bread has browned, add homemade tomato sauce and bring to the boil. Let simmer a couple of minutes and add the flambéed vegetables and squid ink to the pan. Cook for a while, then blend with a stick blender or food processor.

Add the squid to the pan and leave to cook in the sauce, skimming off any froth regularly. When it starts to stick to the pan, it is ready.

PRESENTATION: Serve a helping of squid in ink on a small plate, with croutons as an option.

Hidden: ARATZ

Nuri

INGREDIENTS (MAKES 4 PINTXOS):
4 slices of bread
1 spring onion
4 thick slices of Emmental cheese
Mayonnaise

Cut the spring onion into julienne strips and cook it gently in olive oil until it is caramelised.

Cut 4 slices of bread and toast or grill lightly.

Cut four thick slices of Emmental cheese with more or less the same surface area as the slices of bread, and chop them into tiny cubes. Place them on the bread and cover generously with several tablespoons of mayonnaise.

PRESENTATION: Heat the pintxos (with the bread) for 10 minutes in the oven at 160° C and then spread them with the caramelized shallot.

Optionally, you can decorate this pintxo with half a cherry tomato or with a little goat cheese.

Hidden: ARATZ

Brie Felix

INGREDIENTS:

Brie
Homemade foie gras (see recipe p.186)
Egg
Cornflour
Sunflower oil

FOR THE SWEET AND SOUR SAUCE:

Water
Sugar
Sherry vinegar
Cream

FOR THE SWEET AND SOUR SAUCE: Dissolve the sugar in a little water in a pan and heat it until it caramelises. Add the sherry vinegar and cream. Boil and stir to a creamy consistency. Set aside.

Make balls with the homemade foie and cover them with brie, forming an even larger ball. (The ratio between brie and foie should be 60-40, approximately).

Roll the balls in beaten egg and a little cornflour and fry in sunflower oil.

PRESENTATION: Serve two brie and foie balls on a plate with a few tablespoons of sweet and sour sauce.

This pintxo was specially created for Aratz by Félix Manso, chef at the Bar Restaurant Gaztelumendi-Antxon in Irun. The sweet and sour sauce is an original Aratz recipe.

Haizpe

Plaza Sagastieder, 12. Inchaurrondo

OPENED IN 1995

Esther Vallés is a chef of the first water. Not only can she cook dishes that gourmets come seeking out, such as tripe, pig's ears, kidneys, *ajoarriero*, *sangrecilla* and mushrooms, but she also plays with new ideas, such as cockscombs, the latest product that this constantly inventive cook has been experimenting with. She won the award for Best Renewed Traditional Recipe in 2006, in the prestigious Alcorta-Martin Berasategui competition, with her Txapela pintxo. This victory has meant that she now hobnobs with the best chefs in the province, who from time to time visit this pleasant tavern that has been back in her hands since 2015.

Cockscomb in sauce

INGREDIENTS (MAKES 1 PINCHO):

2 cockscombs
Onion
Garlic
Green pepper
Red pepper
1 teaspoon mild paprika
1 dash dry sherry
Cooking water from the cockscombs

Cook the cockscombs for 45 minutes, then peel. Clean the blood off and remove the thin skin that covers them. Strain and reserve the cooking water.

Sauté the cockscombs for 4 minutes in olive oil and set aside.

Sauté the onion, garlic, green pepper and red pepper, all diced very small. Add the paprika and let it toast slightly, stirring with a wooden spoon.

Add a splash of dry sherry and the cooking water from the cockscombs.

Bring to a boil, add the cockscombs and boil everything together for 10 minutes.

PRESENTATION: Serve the pincho in an individual pottery dish; place the sauce as a base and the two crests, upright, on top.

Hidden: HAIZPE

Txapela

Best traditional recipe in the Alcorta-Martin Berasategui Competition, 2006

INGREDIENTS (MAKES 1 PINCHO):

2 large mushrooms
1 boiled prawn

FOR THE VINAIGRETTE:

Garlic
Green pepper
Red pepper
Parsley
Olive oil
Wine vinegar
Salt

Prepare the vinaigrette by finely chopping all the vegetables, cover them with oil and add a splash of vinegar. Let it marinate for at least 24 hours.

Cook the mushrooms, without the stem, on a griddle gently for 15 minutes, turning often and pricking them to see if they are ready.

PRESENTATION: Place a mushroom hollow side up on a plate. Place the peeled cold prawn on top, add a little salt and fill the hole in the mushroom up with vinaigrette.

Cover with the other mushroom, this time with the hollow side down, and drizzle it with vinaigrette again.

This pincho can be served with a warm vinaigrette.

Hidden: HAIZPE

Tartlet of cod brandade

INGREDIENTS:
Salt cod (soaked overnight)
Prawns
Garlic
Potato
Cream
Salt
Olive oil
Onion
Flour
Tartlet cases

Fry the sliced garlic. When the garlic is golden brown, add the finely chopped cod and sauté. Add the chopped prawns and salt, and cook everything together.

Cut the potatoes into small cubes as if making Spanish omelette and cook gently in olive oil at a low temperature to avoid browning, until nearly cooked.

Once the potato is done, add the cod that has been sautéing with garlic and prawns. The ratio should be roughly twice the amount of cod to potato.

Once everything is cooked, remove it from the heat, let it cool, put everything in a large bowl, add cream and blend in a food processor. Allow to cool.

Cut the onion into rings, add salt, dust with flour and fry.

PRESENTATION: Fill the tartlet cases with the brandade and top with two fried onion rings. Before serving the pincho, heat quickly in the oven or microwave.

Hidden: HAIZPE

Pig's ear in sauce

INGREDIENTS:

Pig's ear
Garlic
Onion
Red pepper
Hot paprika
Cooking water from pig's ear
Salt

Cook the pig's ear for about 30 minutes in boiling salted water and then let it stand. Keep the cooking water.

Chop the ear into squares like tiles (square and flat).

Dice and fry lots of garlic. Add the finely chopped onion and red pepper. Add the paprika and let it toast slightly. Sauté for a few minutes, add the cooking broth and bring to the boil. Add salt and simmer for about 20 minutes, testing halfway through to see if it needs more salt.

Hidden: HAIZPE

Leek supreme

INGREDIENTS:
Garlic
Chicken breast
Leeks (use both white and green parts)
Mayonnaise
Black pepper
Olive oil

Fry the sliced garlic. Chop the leek finely, both white and green parts, and add everything to the frying pan. Sauté over a high heat so that the leeks do not soften too much. Add the black pepper, while the leek sautés.

In another pan, sauté the chicken breast in small cubes with a little olive oil.

Once the chicken is cooked, blend it in a food processor until it becomes a paste.

Add the chicken paste to the pan with the leeks, mix well and cook everything together for five minutes.

Drain the resulting mass well, and after cooling, mix with the mayonnaise.

PRESENTATION: Cut a slice of French bread. Arrange the chicken with leek and mayonnaise on the bread, and decorate with strips of leek, deep-fried until crisp.

Mesón Lugaritz

Avda. Tolosa, 79. Lorea. Tel. 943 21 85 03

OPENED IN 2008

Mesón Lugaritz is a traditional neighbourhood bar that always manages to make you feel at home. Mamen and Mertxe Beraiz manage the kitchen and make sure that the bar is always filled with good food which varies according to that day's market, the season, the suppliers or the intuition of these excellent cooks. Antonio Cano, behind the bar, offers his wisdom on ham and wine and his experience in bartending, as he belongs to the legendary dynasty of the Canos, who have run bars like the Etxebe or the Cervecería Etxeberria, both in Old Quarter of the city.

Iberian ham pintxo

INGREDIENTS:

1 hand-cut slice Iberian ham
1 slice bread
Salted butter
1 slice soft Camembert
Sesame seeds
1 Gernika or Padrón green pepper

Toast the slice of bread. Spread a little salted butter on it.

Place the slice of ham on the toast and the slice of soft Camembert on top.

Toast the sesame seeds in a dry pan and when they are golden brown, remove them. Sprinkle some sesame seeds on the slice of Camembert.

Fry the Gernika or Padrón pepper in olive oil and place it on the top of the pintxo.

PRESENTATION: When serving, before placing the pepper on top, heat the pintxo a little under the grill or in the microwave so that the cheese melts.

Hidden: MESÓN LUGARITZ

Spinach mousse with prawn

INGREDIENTS (MAKES 12 PINTXOS):

4 eggs
1 small carton cream
1 bag spinach leaves
300g peeled prawns
Butter
Garlic
Salt
Pepper
Breadcrumbs
Mayonnaise
Olive oil

Chop the spinach finely and cook for 10 minutes in boiling water with salt and a drop of oil. Drain in a colander and press to get rid of all the water.

Set aside 6 prawns and chop the rest in a food processor. In a frying pan with a little oil and butter, brown the finely chopped garlic and add the chopped prawns. Sauté lightly and set aside.

Mix the cooked spinach and sautéed shrimp in a large bowl with 4 eggs and the carton of cream. Add salt and pepper and whisk lightly.

Butter the insides of 12 individual ramekins and line them with breadcrumbs.

Fill the moulds halfway up with the mixture of spinach and shrimp, and put them in the oven in a bain marie for half an hour at 160° C.

PRESENTATION: Turn the mousses out from the moulds while still hot and place a couple of teaspoons of aioli on top; to prepare this, mix mayonnaise and chopped garlic in a blender.

Garnish each mousse with half a shrimp chopped into small pieces.

Hidden: MESÓN LUGARITZ

Deboned battered pig's trotters

INGREDIENTS:
Pig's trotters
Leek
Carrot
Onion
Parsley
Salt
Flour
Egg
Mild olive oil

Cook the trotters, bones and all, over a low heat in a pan with leek, carrot, onion, parsley and salt, for at least an hour and a half, or until soft.

Let the trotters cool, then debone them carefully. As you debone them, put the meat into a rectangular mould, pressing down to create a terrine.

Once all the trotters are deboned, put the mould in the fridge. In about an hour the gelatine will have set and terrine will harden. If you are in a hurry, you can put it in the freezer to speed up the process.

PRESENTATION: Once the terrine is prepared, cut a portion each time you serve a pintxo, dip it in flour and egg with a pinch of salt, fry in mild olive oil until golden brown and drain on a plate with kitchen tissue to absorb the excess oil before serving it on its own plate.

Hidden: MESÓN LUGARITZ

Mussels in tomato sauce

INGREDIENTS:
Mussels

FOR THE HOMEMADE TOMATO SAUCE:
A ripe tomato
Onion
Green pepper
Bell pepper
Dried ham
Olive oil
A bay leaf
Cayenne pepper

FOR THE HOMEMADE TOMATO SAUCE: Cut the ripe tomato into large pieces and fry with the finely chopped onion, green pepper and bell pepper. Add a small piece of dried ham.

Stir the sauce often; do not blend but leave it thick and chunky. Add a bay leaf and a little cayenne pepper at the last minute.

Clean the mussels and put them in an empty pan. Turn up the heat under the pan and wait until they start opening. Remove the beards and top shells and move the mussels in their lower shell to another pan.

PRESENTATION: Pour the tomato sauce over the mussels, covering them. Turn up the heat and boil for half a minute.

Battered hake

INGREDIENTS:
Hake fillet
Salt
Flour
Egg
Mild olive oil
Lemon or mayonnaise to garnish

Cut the hake into 3-4 cm slices.

Mix the flour, egg and salt in a shallow dish. Dip the hake fillets in this mixture and shallow fry them in mild olive oil over a medium heat.

Fry lightly, then pass the hake to a plate with kitchen tissue to absorb excess oil.

PRESENTATION: Place on another clean plate and serve with a slice of lemon or a little mayonnaise.

Txubillo

Matia 5, rear. El Antiguo. Tel. 943 21 11 38

REOPENED IN 2005

Mesón Txubillo was a classic bar with casserole dishes, stone walls and traditional pintxos until Hitoshi Yoshida and Akari Karube came along in 2005; a Japanese couple who, curiously, met in San Sebastián, in the Luis Irizar cookery school. Hitoshi and Akari, with great knowledge of Japanese and Basque cuisine, decided not to opt for either but to explore a middle way, 'inventing' Basque-Japanese cuisine. This is an exquisite, surprising fusion which gives us multicultural dishes like oxtail cooked with salmon, Ibarra chilli peppers in tempura or their impressive Tuna *tataki*, served only when in season and only when the fish is good enough. An amazing experience.

Warm oyster in sake

INGREDIENTS:

Oysters
1 tsp of sake
1/8 slice of lemon
Coarse salt

Clean the oysters well with a brush under running water.

Place an oyster in a dry pan and heat it until it opens a little. Pour a splash of sake on it. Warm it for half a minute more and remove the shell.

PRESENTATION: Put a little coarse salt on a plate so that the oyster does not fall over and place the oyster with sake on top. Serve with a slice of lemon.

Hidden: TXUBILLO

Bonito tataki

INGREDIENTS:
180 g bluefin tuna
Chopped leek
Chopped basil
Fried garlic
Coarse salt
Virgin olive oil

FOR THE GARNISH:
Onion cut into julienne strips
Chopped chives

FOR THE DRESSING:
Lemon juice
Soy sauce
20 g katsubushi flakes
1.2 litres water
10 cm konbu algae

Clean the konbu algae with a wet cloth.

Fill a saucepan with ½ litre of water and add the konbu algae. Bring to the boil and when boiling, remove the algae from the water. Add 100 ml of water to the pan and add the katsubushi flakes. Let them cook for a few minutes until the water begins to boil again. When it starts to boil, turn off the heat and let it stand for about 5 minutes. Strain the stock with a muslin cloth but do not drain too much, so that the flavour is kept.

Mix 100 ml each of lemon juice, soy sauce and stock. Store in the fridge.

Sear the piece of tuna in a very hot pan and cool it quickly in ice water. Dry the piece well. Cut into 5 mm slices.

PRESENTATION: Put the onion julienne on a plate. Place a slice of tuna on top. Season with coarse salt, 50 ml of the vinaigrette made with lemon juice, katsubushi broth, soy sauce and olive oil. Garnish with chopped chives, chopped leeks and chopped basil. Place a few slices of fried garlic on top.

Always pour the vinaigrette on the tuna first and then the oil, so that oil does not prevent the tuna from absorbing the flavour of the dressing.

Hidden: TXUBILLO

Grilled octopus with vinaigrette, peppers and anchovies

INGREDIENTS:
Octopus
Pickled red, green and yellow peppers
Salted anchovies
Diced tomatoes
Extra virgin olive oil
Rocket leaves
Chopped onion
Allspice

Make a vinaigrette with extra virgin olive oil, the vinegar from the jar of pickled peppers, peppers, salted anchovies, diced tomato and onion.

Boil the octopus for an hour or so, depending on size, and leave to cool, stretching the legs out so that they are straight.

Cut the legs of the octopus lengthwise. Roast them on a grill.

PRESENTATION: Put the vinaigrette on a plate and place the octopus leg on top. Sprinkle with a little coarse salt. Place a leaf of rocket with vinaigrette and a few grains of allspice for garnish.

Hidden: TXUBILLO

Hake cheek tempura

INGREDIENTS:
Hake cheeks
Salt
Green Tea

TEMPURA BATTER:
200 ml cold water
1 egg yolk
100 g flour

Heat a deep fat fryer to 180° C.

In a bowl, whisk the egg yolk with the cold water. Sieve the flour 2 or 3 times and add to the egg mix, still whisking. Do not mix the batter too much, as the gluten will start to appear and this can mean the tempura will not be crispy.

Salt the hake cheeks slightly and dust them lightly with flour. Dip in the tempura batter. Fry at 180° C until the batter is crisp.

PRESENTATION: Season the hake cheeks with the green tea salt. Serve on a small plate.

Grilled marinated salmon

INGREDIENTS:
1 salmon fillet
Sake
Coarse salt
Potato
Onion
Bacon
White wine
Cream
Allspice
Salt and pepper

Marinate the salmon fillet with sake and leave in the refrigerator overnight. The next day, dry the fillet and weigh it. Prepare coarse salt; use 1.5 times the weight of the salmon fillet. Salt the prepared fillet and leave overnight in the fridge, turning it occasionally.

In a saucepan sauté the chopped bacon and add a chopped onion. When well sautéed, add a glass of white wine and let it reduce until almost dry.

Add cream and cook until it has a good flavour.

Sear the salmon fillet and finish it in the oven. Try to take the salmon out when the temperature of the centre reaches 45° C.

PRESENTATION: Put potato on a plate as garnish and place the salmon on top. Sprinkle with allspice.

Vizcacha

Sancho el Sabio, 11. Amara. Tel. 616 52 92 08

REOPENED IN 2011

Javi Ramos spent his youth working in emblematic bars in Renteria, his hometown, and took over the Vizcacha in 2011. Now master of his own bar, he has managed to earn the respect of a loyal clientele by taking care of them, respecting the customers and offering a good service, with a friendly, direct manner and excellent dishes. The Vizcacha is a bar which serves very little food, but what it does serve is top-notch. One thing to look out for is the omelette, a really thick Spanish omelette made with 16 eggs, and succulent and juicy to the last slice. The tripe is also excellent, and they serve freshly cut Iberian ham, good cheese, a small but select wine list and a spectacular range of whiskies.

Chorizo, chicken and ham croquettes

INGREDIENTS:

Chorizo
Chicken breast
Cured ham
Butter
Leek
Milk
Flour
Egg
Breadcrumbs
Oil
Salt

Boil the chorizo and the chicken breast until tender. Chop finely and set aside.

Dice the cured ham and set aside.

Chop the leek finely and sauté it with butter in a large pan. When you have sautéed the leek, add the chopped chorizo, chicken and ham, sauté for a moment and add a pinch of salt. Add the flour and milk and mix briskly to produce a thick béchamel sauce.

Let the béchamel cool, shape it into croquettes, coat them in egg and breadcrumbs and fry in olive oil until crispy on the outside and creamy inside.

Hidden: VIZCACHA

Spanish potato omelette

INGREDIENTS:
16 eggs
4 or 5 potatoes
1 large onion
2 green peppers
Sunflower oil
Olive oil
Salt

Dice the onion and green pepper and fry in oil over a medium heat, until they are well cooked or even slightly burnt.

Cut the potato into slices and fry in oil in another pan over a low heat. Fry the potato slowly, so that it is less cooked than the vegetables. Try to use Monalisa potatoes, which have a wetter texture, which is ideal for Spanish omelette.

In both cases, use a mixture of sunflower oil and olive oil for frying, with more olive oil, in a ratio of 3 to 1, to make the dish less acidic.

Beat 16 eggs in a large bowl and add the vegetables and potatoes. Add salt to taste and cook the Spanish omelette in a non-stick frying pan until it is golden brown outside and slightly runny inside, turning it halfway through cooking.

Hidden: VIZCACHA

Tripe á la Dosi

INGREDIENTS:
Beef tripe
Beef snout
Chorizo
Cured ham
Onion
Tomato
Chilli pepper
Olive oil
Flour
Bay leaf
Salt

Clean the tripe, cut it into pieces and cook it with the beef snout for an hour in a pressure cooker.

Meanwhile, make the sauce: dice the onion and sauté it in olive oil. Add the peeled, diced tomato and the sliced chilli pepper, and continue sautéing until well cooked. Add a little water or some of the cooking water from the tripe if it is done, then add a bay leaf and simmer to reduce for 15-20 minutes. Remove the bay leaf and blend in a food processor.

Cut up the ham and chorizo and sauté them in a pan with a little olive oil. Add them to the sauce.

Finally, add the tripe and snout to the sauce and cook everything for an hour over a low heat so that the gelatine from the tripe thickens the sauce and the flavours blend well.

This dish is best if allowed to stand overnight.

Hidden: VIZCACHA

Beef snout in sauce

INGREDIENTS:
Beef snout
Spring onion
Garlic
Carrot
Leek
Tomato
Parsley
White wine
Stock
Flour
Egg

Cook the snouts in the pressure cooker for half an hour. When soft, dip in egg, dust with flour and fry in olive oil until golden brown.

To make the sauce, finely chop the leek, spring onion, garlic and carrot and sauté them in olive oil. Add the peeled, diced tomatoes, and continue sautéing until everything is soft. Add a little cooking stock and reduce the sauce for 15-20 minutes. Blend in a food processor.

Add the snouts to the sauce and cook everything for 10-15 minutes over a low heat to blend flavours. Finally, sprinkle everything with freshly chopped parsley.

Serve the snouts as a pintxo or small serving.

This dish is best if allowed to stand overnight.

Hidden: VIZCACHA